BOWIEODYSSEY74

Also by Simon Goddard

BOWIEODYSSEY74

SIMONGODDARD

OMNIBUS PRESS

London / New York / Paris / Sydney / Copenhagen / Berlin / Madrid / Tokyo

Note to the Reader: The following narrative takes place in 1974 and contains language and prevailing attitudes of the time which some readers may find offensive. The publishers wish to reassure that all such instances are there specifically for reasons of historical social context in order to accurately describe the period concerned.

Copyright © 2024 Omnibus Press
(A division of the Wise Music Group
14–15 Berners Street, London, W1T 3LJ)

Paperback cover image and endpapers by Michael Ochs Archives/Getty Images
Hardback cover image by Bettmann/Getty Images
Cover designed by Fabrice Couillerot
Art direction and picture research by Simon Goddard

Paperback ISBN 978-1-9158-4103-2
Hardback ISBN 978-1-9158-4104-9

Every effort has been made to trace the copyright holders of the photographs in this book but one or two were unreachable. We would be grateful if the photographers concerned would contact us.

A catalogue record for this book is available from the British Library.

Typeset by Evolution Design & Digital Ltd (Kent)
Printed in Poland
www.omnibuspress.com

BOWIECONTENTS74

'If you're gonna go potty, you may as well go potty in style.'

MIKE, *STARDUST*, 1974

PROLOGUE

'EVERY TUESDAY – DAVID BOWIE NIGHT'

DARKNESS! NOT JUST the black of night but the black of winter's day. Coal strikes, power cuts and the emergency three-day week. Highways of unlit lampposts like petrified trees. Unattended toddlers eating rat poison in the gloom of candlelit shops. Blank railway departure boards. The telly being closed down every night on the stroke of half ten. Tory minister Patrick Jenkin telling the nation to save energy by 'cleaning your teeth in the dark'. Slashed hours, thinning pay packets and housewives wailing 'if this carries on, we'll be living on bread and scrape!' Cold beds, empty bellies and misery. Everywhere, utter misery.

Except in Jilly's.

'UNAFFECTED BY POWER CUTS'.

Four magic words in January 1974. And three more.

'DAVID BOWIE NIGHT'.

Like it says, every Tuesday, in a poky club down a pokier side street a few yards from Manchester Piccadilly station where it launched last October promising discount beer and 'Free Gifts For Best Bowie Outfits'.

Jilly's might be the first 'David Bowie Night' anywhere in the country, but it won't be the last. Because the Head of State is still the Queen, the Prime Minister, by a slipping fingernail, is still Edward Heath, but this,

1

now, is David Bowie's England. And Scotland, and Wales, and Northern Ireland. Rip up all flags and rewrite all anthems.

RULE BOWIETANNIA!

Not because of the millions of records, magazines, T-shirts, badges and posters on bedroom walls from Truro to the Trossachs. Donny Osmond, who has a bigger fan club, has all that too. So does Gary Glitter, who last year sold more singles. But hunt high and low and you won't anywhere find a 'Donny Osmond Night' or a 'Gary Glitter Night'. Not even a 'Slade Night', and they're still number 1. Because they're just pop stars.

David Bowie is something else. Something more than so much vinyl, paper, tin and cloth. He's an evolution, an attitude, a posture, a whole other human existence. A new pair of eyes to see the world with different colours.

And he is *everywhere*.

In Essex salon windows, handwritten signs advertise the cost of a 'David Bowie Cut And Dye' for men *and* women.

One hairdresser in Staffordshire claims 'at least 60 per cent of our business is now Bowie cuts, tints and colours'.

Jewellers down the Elephant & Castle are growing accustomed to barrow boys queueing out of their door to have the one ear pierced 'like David Bowie'.

In East Yorkshire, a teenager is fined six quid in damages for taking a 2p coin to the toilet walls of Beverley train station and scratching the name 'David Bowie'.

In Coventry, a mugging victim describes his assailant to detectives as 'wearing a Crombie coat with a David Bowie haircut'.

The same things are not happening on account of Alvin Stardust.

Beyond henna, hoop earrings, juvenile courts, Warwickshire police photofits and a regular Tuesday night in a Manchester disco, David Bowie is a social oxygen changing the way people move, think and feel.

Carol is a 21-year-old salon assistant in Wolverhampton. She wears six-inch silver platform boots, cut-off jeans and a studded top. Her fingernails are blue, her hair is orange and at weekends she goes out with a red lightning flash across her face. 'I feel sexier when I dress like this,' she says. Her boyfriend, Billy, who has a dyed-green moustache agrees. 'The Bowie look really turns people on.'

Anna is a 15-year-old convent school girl from Preston. She lives, breathes and sleeps David Bowie. She just doesn't eat David Bowie. But then Anna doesn't eat anything. She sees her body in the mirror and his pictures on her wall and realises the only metamorphosis from one to the other involves retching over a toilet bowl the moment she's finished her tea. One day, very soon, she, too, will be famous when she runs away from home only to turn up lost and lonely 200 miles away across the Irish Sea in a cafeteria in Ballynahinch, all six-and-a-half stone of her carrying little more than a carefully folded picture of her idol. Finding herself the star of one of the first national tabloid stories to include the words 'anorexia nervosa'. Side by side with the name 'David Bowie'.

John is a 33-year-old singer-songwriter from Liverpool. He understands the impact of David Bowie better than most. Ten years ago, that of his own band wasn't so dissimilar. 'Well, Bowie is a *threat* in a way,' says Lennon in his first press interview of 1974. 'If you get Bowie on TV and somebody switches on in Ohio or Bradford and they see this person looking out at them, it's going to affect their whole way of life. He doesn't have to say, "Power to the people, right on." He is the message in himself. It's like holding a mirror up to society.'

David, the mirror, the world, his reflection. Even in the pitch black of northern midwinter, dappling like moonbeams on water as they glint through the shadows down Gore Street towards the threshold of Jilly's. Where, inside, lipstick and hairspray are all the valour lathe workers, shopgirls and the unemployably unemployed need to transform into a fantastic menagerie, all shapes, all sizes, all shedded insecurities, every one of them pretending tomorrow the hell of reality won't still be there to kick them in the face like a hobnailed boot. So, tonight, in heaven, they dance in glass slippers.

But outside, always, that darkness. Shrouding. Unshifting.

And ever so slowly thickening . . .

ONE

SEEN AT NIGHT, especially on a freezing January night like this, it looks like a house where The Devil might live. Even by day, it still looks like a house where The Devil might live. As if a Transylvanian castle had been snatched from the slopes of the Carpathian Mountains and incongruously plonked between the Queen Anne mansions flanking Holland Park. Its stained-glass windows set in Saxon arches could *almost* be those of a church, if only the lack of light within didn't seem so godless. Its protruding carved gargoyle gutter spout could *almost* be funny, if only its face wasn't so genuinely frightening. Its dominant cylindrical turreted tower could *almost* be that in a fairy tale, if only the prospect for any poor maiden locked away there didn't appear so unrescuably bleak. Because beyond demons, vampires, mad scientists and masked phantoms, it is impossible to believe so eerie a fortress could be anyone's *home*.

Outside its front gate a black cast-iron Victorian lamppost begs for a swirling Ripper fog. Standing beneath it, having just stepped out of the back of a limousine, is a thin figure wearing an ankle-length coat and a flat-brimmed bolero hat.

Silhouetted under this lamppost, in that hat, and that coat, it looks exactly like the image on the poster of a film currently breaking records in America for the amount of people willing to queue for hours on end just to vomit, faint or run screaming from the theatre before the credits have rolled.

5

Until the silhouette becomes two and any similarity is lost.

The second is hatless at one end, stiletto-heeled at the other, the body between swathed in fur. Together, the two shapes step away and walk through the iron gates, up the nine stone steps to a dimly lit porch with heavy doors set with crown glass. Before they can press the bell, the right door creaks open to expose a disarmingly undevilish little man in a gabardine suit and matching grey tie: his shoes polished, chin smooth, back and sides short, and manners gently simpering.

'Ah, Mr and Mrs Bowie! So *very* pleased to meet you.'

He outstretches a hand.

Mr Bowie shakes it with icy fingers. 'Hello,' he sniffs, the voice no warmer.

Then Mrs Bowie. Her grip firmer, her greeting firmer still.

'JUST FROM OUTSIDE THIS LOOKS *FAAABULOUS!*'

The suit takes a step backwards.

'Please,' he smiles, stiffly pointing an open palm through an inner bronze door where they walk as instructed into a hallway, its soft golden lighting allowing their host a better look at his clients.

Mr Bowie, David, just turned 27. A waxy smooth face, the smoother for having no eyebrows, and ghostly pale, the paler for being framed by loose bangs of russet hair tickling his collar and a hunter green hat he never removes. His eyes appear to be contrasting colours and a large golden hoop, big enough to hang heavy curtains, dangles from his left earlobe. He sniffs more than he speaks, and the suit quickly reaches the conclusion that this gentleman may not be especially all that well.

Mrs Bowie, Angela, 24. A tight strawberry-blonde perm crowning a searchlight smile, blue eyes flickering with the not unfriendly but very definite warning to do-as-I-ask-or-be-verbally-guillotined. Her accent is the finishing school American of tragic Fitzgerald heroines and matches her polite if outwardly theatrical manner. The suit assumes her to be some sort of actress, and in the sense that her life has become one long exhausting performance he isn't altogether wrong.

Otherwise, he has no idea. Only a very vague understanding that they have *something* to do with 'the popular music business', as one of the girls in the city offices of Gross Fine & Krieger Chalfen informed him when given the viewing. Maybe if he was the sort of chap who subscribed to *Time* magazine, then he'd know from the latest issue that the green-hatted gentleman before him wearing a very elegant matching full-length mohair coat with a leather satchel slung over his shoulder has just been voted 'The Tenth Worst Dressed *Woman* of 1973' by Tinsel Town's queeniest bitch, designer Mr Blackwell. Or if he was the sort who buttered his morning crumpets over a letterbox-fresh copy of *The Sun*, where he'd have seen the 5 foot 9 inch blonde presently towering over him only a few days ago looking even more Amazonian dressed in a Wonder Woman outfit complete with lasso. But being more of a *Punch* and *Telegraph* fellow with an ear for Brahms, he is sadly ignorant, albeit satisfied enough that Mr and Mrs Bowie arrived here in a chauffeured Daimler still on the clock and parked waiting outside. They clearly have money. Just as well.

'So, as I explained on the telephone,' he begins, 'Mr Harris isn't here just now but he's very happy to let you look around in his abs–'

'DAVID, LOOK!' Angie interrupts, arm catapulting up to the minstrel gallery above their heads.

'ISN'T IT LIKE HADDON HALL?'

David nods, wagging his hat brim.

'OUR OLD HOME IN BECKENHAM,' she enlightens the suit. 'FROM THE SAME PERIOD, LATE VICTORIAN. EXCEPT THIS REALLY IS . . . OH MY!'

Her eyes chase David's down to the tiled mosaic labyrinth beneath their feet where Theseus grapples with the Minotaur.

'*Exquisite*, isn't it,' sighs the suit. 'The whole house is the lifetime's culmination of its architect, William Burges, the greatest exponent of the Gothic revival style. This was his last home. His *pièce de résistance*, if you will.'

David inhales the décor, sniff by sniff, brick by brick, head twitching up to the high vaulted ceiling decorated with gold stars and mythical creatures, and down the walls painted to look like the stonework of a medieval castle, the twin towering frescoes of the sun and moon gods, the polished marble pillars with Corinthian crowns, the opposite doorway with two gold lionheads biting either side of its frame.

'Burges died here in 1881,' says the suit with the tiniest tilt of his head. 'Since then it's been in several hands, up until a very brief and unfortunate period when it fell into disrepair. But in the past ten years there's been a great deal of restoration work, including by Mr Harris. For a property almost one hundred years old it truly is in remarkable condition. Please, allow me to show you the dining room.'

He leads them between the lionheads into a pink and green marble paradise, ribboned around all four walls by a tiled frieze depicting a procession of English folk heroes. Above, painted on the recessed ceiling, the sun, the planets and the twelve signs of the zodiac.

'HA!' laughs Angie, craning her neck. 'IT'S JUST LIKE TRAMP!'

In the centre of the room, a second zodiac adorns an enormous round dining table fit for the court of King Arthur. David glides a hand across its shiny surface, picturing instead the court of King Bowie. Himself, back to the stained-glass window, maybe raising a goblet to Mick Jagger, sat on David's left beside his wife Bianca. On his right, stroking his knee, one of his many lovers – Ava, or Amanda, or even Angie herself. Further down, his live-in wardrobe whiz Freddie, or his new pal 'Bill', the beat poet William Burroughs, sharing junkie wisdom, cigarettes and dirty jokes with Marianne Faithfull. And somewhere, sat on somebody's knee or maybe perched alone on a high cushion, his two-and-a-half-year-old son, Zowie, tracing the tabletop outline of Scorpio's pincers with his little finger, quietly listening to the mystifying adult hubbub, nostrils flaring with so many strange perfumes.

'These are all Burges's original fittings. Apart from the table, which Mr Harris commissioned.' The suit clears his throat. 'If, when you're ready, you'd like to follow me?'

Room after room the reveries continue, each more absurd in their ornate beauty. Ceiling cupids, carved alphabets entwined in Gothic foliage, golden chimneypieces, an altar-sized mantelpiece based on the Tower of Babel, embossed flowers, wall frieze after wall frieze as painstakingly detailed as the Bayeux Tapestry, a stained-glass Joan of Arc, encaustic tiling, painted wall cabinets so stunning you'd believe they'd been plundered from some ancient Flemish cathedral. David and Angie's senses can't begin to digest so much finesse and finery but on they wander like fleas trapped inside a Fabergé egg, following their guide up the tower's spiral stairs to the upper floors audibly groaning with so much marble upon marble, ceilings studded with mirror-encrusted stars, frieze upon frieze of plants, fishes and butterflies, sculptures of mermaids, monkeys and storybook giants. Maybe like the one who must have eaten the entire Uffizi gallery before throwing it back up in W14.

'GOD, IT'S INCREDIBLE!'

'Yes,' sniffs David, inspecting some fleurs-de-lys. 'It is.'

The little suit rubs his chin. 'Of *course* . . .' he says, pausing for effect, 'it is Grade 1 listed. Truly a once-in-a-lifetime property, one of a kind. Hence the asking price.'

Angie's gaze pins him like a stapler. 'REMIND ME?'

'As I think we already discussed, we're looking in the region of . . .'

He ceremonially breaks her stare, looking down to brush something invisible from his cuff. He clears his throat. Their eyes reconnect.

'. . . Three hundred.'

'THOUSAND?'

'Pounds,' he nods, not quite blushing. 'Yes.'

David's face doesn't flicker.

'We have – oh, *naturally* – we have had *other* interested parties. But, well, of course, we're very keen such a house is bought by the right, well, *custodian* shall we say.' The suit twitches his birdlike eyes between them. 'You yourself, Mr Bowie, are you in the process of selling?'

'No,' says David, distracted. 'Renting.' He sniffs. 'In Chelsea, not far.'

'OH, BUT WE WANT TO BUY!'

'Mmm. Like my wife says. We want to buy,' hums David. 'In London. West London.' Then his lips contort in the first fanged smile since he walked through the front door.

'You see, what we're really looking for is a home.'

The smile strains at the corners. 'Yes,' he adds, less certain.

Another sniff and it's gone.

'Mmm. A home.'

THEY'RE NOT QUITE BACK in the limousine when David sparks his first cigarette, the smoke billowing in the frosty air like dragon's breath. The clunk of a door, a low mechanical rumble, and the car gently swings along the curving road. David twists his head around for a last look, the outline of the strange old house only just visible against the starless evening.

'NURSERY. . . ZOWIE . . . PARTIES . . .'

Beside him, Angie is talking. To David, to her window, to the world outside scrolling by like a carousel. He picks up the occasional word, but her voice is already background noise to his own crashing symphony of thought.

Home.

David's had many in his short life so far. Stansfield Road. Canon Road. Clarence Road. Plaistow Grove. Clareville Grove. Foxgrove Road. Haddon Hall. Vale Court. Oakley Street . . .

Haddon Hall.

His last real *home*. The one Angie found for them in the autumn of '69. The ground-floor flat where David proposed to her long-distance by telephone, where they spent their wedding night, where their son was conceived along with most of the songs that have made David so famous he was forced to leave there last summer for his own safety. Ever since he's been homeless. Never houseless, but homeless all the same. An occupant, not a resident.

'. . . BIANCA . . . STUDIO . . . TONY . . .'

Angie is still talking as David, still half-listening, stubs out one cigarette and lights another. He quietly puffs and more quietly ponders.

The house they've just seen, the Tower House on Melbury Road. Could *that* be home?

It's true it reminded him of Haddon Hall, albeit preposterously grander. But it took Angie and David themselves to transform the creaky shell of Haddon Hall with paint, rugs and their combined magpie eyes for curious antiques. The Tower House defies any attempt at adornment. It's a ready-made masterpiece by Botticelli, every minute detail painted carefully in place, asking only that they complete the picture by draping over its furniture like Venus and Mars.

Could they?

David shuts his eyes and tries to imagine. Sitting in the library, strumming a guitar, his voice echoing up the chimney of the Tower of Babel. Waking up and seeing stars and fish, his every manoeuvre between the sheets observed by a carved wooden mermaid. Peering out through stained glass at the street outside, counting the days until *they* track him down and it starts all over again: the pressing of the doorbell, the desperate notes through the letterbox, every brick on the front wall defaced with his name in ink, lipstick or penknife scratches. But then how and *where* else are the gods of rock'n'roll supposed to live on mortal soil?

Take Elton, with his relatively modest modern mansion in Surrey, 'Hercules'. Or Rod, with a less modest 32-room mansion in 17 acres of ground near Royal Ascot, complete with indoor swimming pool, Italianate garden and enough garage space for his Lamborghini, Roller and new Merc with a telly in the back. Or Marc, currently restoring a listed rectory in Herefordshire to its original seventeenth-century splendour. Or David's mate and Chelsea neighbour, Mick, with his Georgian townhouse on Cheyne Walk *and* his country estate, Stargroves, on the Hampshire borders. Or even their mutual friend, Ronnie Wood, proud owner of 'The Wick', an eighteenth-century Thameside mansion in Richmond with 20 rooms, including its own basement recording studio where he's recently had David and Mick, together, jamming at midnight on a dirty new groove called 'It's Only Rock 'N' Roll'. And he's *only* the guitarist in the Faces.

David is David Bowie. The new King of England. Four of last year's Top 20 best-selling LPs were his, including *Aladdin Sane*, pipped only by the compilation soundtrack to the David Essex film *That'll Be the Day*. Because no artist – not Elton, not Rod, not the Rolling Stones, not the Faces – sold more albums than he did in 1973. And yet there they are in their lovely listed buildings, each with more rooms than half a dozen Cluedo boards, and their cooks, and their cleaners, and their chauffeurs named Cyril, and their vast acreages, and their rose gardens, and their horses and dogs, and their fleets of Rolls-Royces in every colour, and their swimming pools, indoors and out, and their home studios, and their games rooms, and their croquet lawns, and their pictures in the newspapers posing in their driveways like the landed gentry of a Gainsborough painting, to each their rock'n'roll manor born.

And, meanwhile, here's David, his driver pulling up in a quiet residential street off the King's Road, next to a rented house that, while no slum, is too tall, too thin and too busy with guests treating it like some 24/7 Soho massage parlour. Too nothing like his *home*.

Angie is already out of the car and up the steps with the keys in her hand. On the backseat, David doesn't move.

'DAVID?'

She turns, halfway through the front door. '*DAVID?* ARE YOU COMING IN?'

He sniffs, a bony knuckle lightly tapping his window. Then he slides along the seat to the kerbside, shuts his door, follows her inside, heads straight up the long thin stairs to the bathroom, removes his hat in front of the mirror and from inside his coat pulls a small vial of white powder and a spindly metallic spoon.

Outside his window, in the skies above Chelsea, the coagulating darkness deepens . . .

HER EYES SNAG ON THE WORDS like a fish on a hook. Heart flipping, breath quickening, she reads it for a second time.

'*Drool over David . . .*'

Then, with an inward sigh, the line slackens and she wriggles free.

'*. . . Bowie.*'

Not her David. Not the one hanging above every side of her bed in posters as big as the sheets, the face of an ageless man-boy with golden brown hair, an apple-pie smile and jewel-box eyes sparkling with a love sublime. Not the one she saw in concert at Wembley last March, the Brownie Instamatic trembling between her then-13-year-old fingers as it periscoped above the girls squashed in front to snap a spotlit figure so pristine white he looked beamed-down. Not the one whose daydreaming voice is the sole vibrator of her Dansette bar one Osmonds LP and two budget hits compilations. Not the one whose fan club is 75p the richer for her membership in return for a glossy A4 folder containing a fact sheet, one poster, two photos and several blank sheets of pink writing paper with his face stamped on top above the words 'I think I love you'. Not the star of her dreams when welcome sleep falls, nor her hot midnight shame when it refuses. *O Lord, forgive me my sins just as you forgave Peter's denial and those who crucified you!* No, not *her* David.

'*. . . Bowie.*'

Her deflated glance slides away from the cover of *Valentine* along the remaining shelf of teenage magazines. Donny on one, Gary on another, the rest with pretty girls in winter woollens. A rare week when David Cassidy isn't anywhere to be seen. One last double-check, then Bernadette walks out of the shop, the same change jingling in her purse as when she walked in.

The winter air stabs fresh colour to her cheeks. Tightening her coat, she weaves back towards her estate, along dusky Stockwell streets that have been her new home since the week before Christmas. The very streets – not that she knows, not that she'd much care if she did – where droolsome David Bowie was born 27 years ago this month, on a house on Stansfield Road, a mere schoolgirl's skip of 600 yards from her own family's flat in Crowhurst House. Her short move south from Vauxhall just means a different bus stop to school, if still the same school, a different bedroom, if still the same posters, a different newsagent, if still the same magazines. And a different church, if still the same God.

Amen.

Aged 14, Bernadette believes. She's a good daughter of parents from the Old Country: Peter, her father, from County Wexford, and her mother, Bridget, from Dublin's fair city, hair in a bun and the crucified Saviour on a gold chain round her neck. And herself, baptised none more sacred a name than Bernadette, Saint of Our Lady of Lourdes, and *The Song of Bernadette*. And even if the song of this Bernadette is 'The Puppy Song' by David Cassidy, she still believes. Between the Sister teachers at her Battersea convent school, Mass every Sunday morning, the framed picture of her confirmation on the mantelpiece and the dull shine of her mother's cross over the dinner table, she cannot not believe. *In the Lord, the giver of life.* Except to *really* believe in the man up above means she must also believe in the other. Down below.

But that's why she has her David. Her guardian angel. Always over her shoulder in the mirror as she brushes on her make-up, his voice shuddering the speaker on the bedroom floor beside her, just as he is right now.

'*Life is much too beautiful to live it all alone . . .*'

Not yet teatime and the winter sun has sunk. The faint smell of hot cooking fat creeps from the kitchen under her door as the song ends, the runout crackles and the arm returns to its rest. She flips the record up off the turntable and carefully places it back in its sleeve, pondering which other to play next. *The Partridge Family Notebook* or *Rock Me Baby*? Not that she's in any rush to choose. At 14, Bernadette has her whole much too beautiful life ahead of her.

Outside her window, in the skies above Stockwell where she sends her prayers, the suffocating darkness sneers . . .

TWO

'SOONER OR LATER.'

That was the title of the script when it first fell through the letterbox of his Sussex mansion named Whaphams. Like the sound of a thick parcel dropping on a doormat.

Whap-hams!

Terry hadn't asked for it, so when he hobbled over on his crutch to pick it up he had no idea what was inside. If it hadn't been for the inertia of his convalescence, he probably wouldn't have read the bleedin' thing. But when you're recovering from a car crash you spend a lot of time sat on your arse with nothing to do except check the markets in the *FT*. Sooner or later he knew he'd end up reading *Sooner or Later*.

He almost didn't. Before he'd flipped the first page his agent rang and told him if he fancied the role then the director, Mr Apted, would insist on him filming a screen test. Insulted, Terry returned it, unread.

A few days later, a familiar thud echoed down the hall from his letterbox.

Whap-hams!

They'd sent it back. That's when the begging phone calls from a very apologetic producer named Mr Puttnam began.

'Listen, me old cock,' sighed Terry, 'I'm not doing it.'

It was pride, mostly. He knew he wasn't first choice for the part. So did everyone else who read the bleedin' papers.

'*Ringo Starr has turned down a big film role because, he says, he couldn't face Beatlemania again.*'

It was always Ringo's role since he'd starred in the first film and this was the sequel. But as the ex–Beatle told the *Mirror*: 'Having lived through the madness once, I couldn't experience it a second time. It's too close to home.'

Reading the script, Terry understood why. It was a very well written but equally sordid piece about fame, success, egos, exploitation, drugs and madness. The kind of story that gave the music business, *his* business, a bad name.

'Don't bleedin' well ask me again! I'm not doing it, cock.'

So he keeps telling Mr Puttnam, and so Mr Puttnam keeps ringing back for the same fob-off. About how Terry is done with acting, especially after the crash, even if he's now out of plaster and able to get about without a stick. But he still has a jerking limp so unless it's *Richard III* they're offering, what's the bleedin' point?

'I'm a businessman now.'

Like he says. A *businessman*. An artist manager and record producer with more than enough on his plate looking after his pet protégé. His boy.

In a funny way it was the boy's fault he'd had the car crash in the first place. He'd driven up to Bedfordshire to see him support Procol Harum and, as he often does, Terry bitterly criticised his performance.

'Too many amateurs in this business. Not enough pros.'

When he wants to be, or rather when he *has* to be, Terry is no less of a hardnosed bastard than the character Mr Puttnam wants him to play in the film he still doesn't want to make. Just like he knew he had to be that night in Dunstable when he walked in the dressing room and fired the boy's backing band, brooding as he drove home how he was going to make a pro out of the boy even if it killed him. And in the same breath lost control of his Ford Granada and skidded across a garage forecourt into an oak tree.

WHAP-HAMS!

They dragged him from the wreckage with serious abdominal injuries, a broken arm and a broken leg. The doctors said if he hadn't been wearing a seatbelt he'd very definitely be dead, and in his first interview with the papers from his hospital bed – cut, bandaged and still groggy on medication – Terry made sure he thanked 'Clunk Click' safety campaigner Jimmy Savile. 'For saving my life.'

At least it wasn't entirely in vain. With Terry's guidance, and new musicians, his boy got better. So much so by Christmas he'd finally made a star out of him. All it took was a lucky TV break, a Pierrot costume, white greasepaint, a skull cap and the maudlin banjo scat of 'The Show

Must Go On'. Now he's currently number 2 in the charts and tipped by *The Sun* as the new Face of Pop for 1974.

'This will be Leo Sayer's year just as surely as 1973 belonged to David Bowie.'

A bold prediction, seconded by *Melody Maker*. Strange as it may be that anyone could think David Bowie would ever be usurped by a squawky little man in a clown outfit. Still, nobody, least of all Leo with his odd quips about being a cross between 'an egomaniac' and 'the village idiot', is more certain of Leo's lasting success than his boss.

'I think he is potentially the best singer in the world,' predicts Terry. 'If I ever thought he was just a pop singer I wouldn't want to know. I want Leo to be important. I don't want him to be bottom of the bill to anybody, not even if it's Bob Dylan or Elvis Presley.'

The queerest thing about all of this being that the same rags-to-riches starmaking business Terry's so preoccupied with when it comes to his Leo is exactly what the bleedin' film script is all about. Which is what Mr Puttnam keeps telling him. Over and over and over again.

'You *know* this story. You've *lived* it . . .'

It's true. He has, from both sides, as a manager and a pop star, one of Britain's very first, a thousand pizzicato plucks ago. Fifteen years, in fact, since Terry Nelhams first topped the pops as Adam Faith.

'. . . And you *know* you know this character. I've fixed it so you won't even have to do a screen test anymore. If you want it, it's yours. *Please?'*

'Oh, Christ! Awlright! Awlright! If it means you'll stop bleedin' ringing me every day, I'll bleedin' well do it!'

'Really?'

'*Yes!* There, I've said it. Awlright? So you can hang up now, cock.'

The ecstatic producer does, shortly after Terry learns they'll be shooting from early February as soon as the lead actor gets back from America where he's been promoting his own blossoming pop career.

'Oh,' adds Mr Puttnam, 'and there's been a change of title.'

'Good,' says Terry. '*Sooner or Later*'s bleedin' crap. What is it?'

And so Mr Puttnam tells him. Everything the script has to say about the irresistible lustre and fickle illusion of fame boiled down to a single word.

Because if anyone had to film a tragedy about an English rock'n'roll idol in modern Bowietannia, why would they call it anything else?

'*Stardust.'*

THREE

THE ALL-DAY LINE outside the cinema behind Bloomingdale's isn't quite as long as last week. But then last week it was the only theatre in New York showing *The Exorcist*. When the queue of students, housewives, bank clerks, bored spinsters, giggling couples and nervous teens praying they looked old enough to be admitted stretched two blocks back to Second Avenue, sometimes coming to blows over skipped places and push-ins, while the cold and desperate lit trashcan bonfires as the temperature shivered to a frostbiting ten below zero. But it's still long.

So are the other newer queues, one four blocks north at the Beekman, another four blocks west at the Paris, another across the other side of the park at the Paramount. Critics, psychologists and clergymen all have their theories as to the root of this R-rated hysteria: strategic Hollywood exploitation, a mass social bonding ritual, a renewed need for a belief in some divine power of good against evil. But whatever the cause, the tally of human souls still standing in line, some for their second, third or even fourth time, amounts to the same undeniable truth. The Devil has taken Manhattan.

Five blocks south of Cinema 1 where it opened on Boxing Day, where ever since the disinfectant reek of freshly mopped vomit hangs in the air like Beelzebub's own fart, a very different smell, one that could almost be brimstone if it wasn't less obviously smouldering Havana leaf, asphyxiates the potted plants of an office on Park Avenue.

Tracing this odour to its source would lead any curious nostrils to the glowing ashy tip of a fat brown cylinder poking from between the lips of a tanned head with a broad nose and steady eyes which blink with the calm of a frog on a lilypond patiently awaiting its next insect to buzz within gobbling distance. A head that, even were it horned, would be hard to tell for its smooth but dense topiary of black curls. A head that has yet to subject itself to the sensory overload of *The Exorcist* for the simple reason that this is the head of Tony Defries. And Defries is not a man who waits in line.

The leather-inlaid desk in front of him, big enough to accommodate a sizeable train set, is instead home to his preferred toys of several telephones, a fat square glass ashtray, a wooden cigar box, a silver desktop lighter, a silver blotter, a silver letter tray, a selection of paperweights of varying geometric shapes and an untidy spread of dockets, letters and torn telexes laid out before him like a poker hand. The winning hand as he sees it. But then Defries is not a man who acknowledges loss.

Anyone else dealt the same cards might think otherwise. Urgent demands for unpaid studio bills. Legal threats over rent arrears. Rejected licensing agreements. Memos about disrupted schedules due to UK pressing plant restrictions and the vinyl shortage crisis. This week's *Billboard* with only one of his acts in either Top 100, and then only at number 45. The latest volley in divorce proceedings from Mrs Defries. Not so much a hand as a crippled foot.

This is not what Defries sees. Through the low-lying tabletop haar of his smoke, the letters and numbers miraculously rearrange. Jokers becomes aces, twos become kings and every suit is a diamond. Because why worry about the battles of expenditure when you've won the war of income? The Park Avenue office, the East 55th penthouse, the country retreat in Connecticut, the chauffeured limousine between all three, the beautiful younger girlfriend, the finest imported Cuban cigars, the management of David Bowie. And all of his fortune.

That's why Defries has just the one simple plan for 1974. The same plan he's had ever since he started winning in 1972. Sell more Bowie.

Sell him to a Hollywood studio for a picture deal. Sell him as rumours of a Broadway musical about Ziggy Stardust and another in the West End based on *Nineteen Eighty-Four*. Sell him in coliseums and sports arenas from Anaheim to Atlanta. Sell him on radio jingles, TV spots and high above the traffic on Sunset Strip. Sell him like Hershey's and Coca-Cola. Sell him not by the box but by the pallet. Sell him not by the pallet but by the truck. Sell him not by the truck but by the convoy. Sell him not by the convoy but by the warehouse. Then build a bigger warehouse and sell him all over again.

Sell him as a doppelgänger. Sell him as Mick Ronson, the Bowie who isn't quite Bowie but his former guitarist in The Spiders From Mars. Sell him in Ronson's imminent solo debut, gasping on the life support of three 'new Bowie tracks' even as it proves that no magician's assistant, however gifted, is fully capable of sawing themselves in half.

Sell him by association. Sell him as Dana Gillespie, David's old girlfriend whose revamped public image for 1974 seems to be 'Klondike whorehouse, 1898'. Sell him in Dana's first album for Mainman featuring two demos he produced for her three years ago, including his own 'Andy Warhol', tacked on as Bowie bait to as boring a record anyone could ever try to flog in a sleeve straight out of the Ann Summers catalogue.

Sell him as another shyster's confidence trick. Sell him in their 40-foot square billboard currently hanging over Times Square showing the toppled alabaster statute of a naked young man with an androgynous face and spindly piano fingers. Sell him as '*Jerry Brandt presents an album by Jobriath*'. Sell him in their ballyhoo of 'Jobriath is a true fairy', and their dukes up of 'David Bowie has taken his best shot – he's tacky and he can't pirouette and he can't move and he's rigid and he's scared to death.' Sell him in the dyslexia of Marc Bolan who calls him 'Joe Braith'. Then sell Bowie as the original, accept no imitations.

It's the golden rule and the bottom line. *The product must always be in the state of being sold.* Even now, as the telex machine whirrs, clicks and spits out more bad news from London, Defries has the game all in hand. Just by sitting here. Just by rolling the smoke around his mouth and gently tapping his ash. Just by doing nothing except being the main man of Mainman. Always in a state of selling Bowie.

Below his window on the snowy streets of Manhattan, one of the 200 buses of the Metropolitan Transport Authority network advertising Jobriath on its side ploughs uptown through the slush. Passing yet more people making their way to sit in the dark and watch a little girl spew 'YOUR MOTHER SUCKS COCKS IN HELL!'

★

WHERE EXACTLY *IS* HELL? As Mephistopheles told Faustus, any place that isn't heaven. Maybe a back garden in Loughton, where a policeman is burying the wife he first strangled, then hung in his loft overnight like an ageing ham while he made love to his mistress in the bedroom below. Or a parked car in Highgate where an architect wakes up one morning to find witchcraft-crazed vandals have stolen a 100-year-old corpse from the local cemetery, chopped off its head and left it sitting in his passenger seat. Ask the vicar in Chalk Farm with licence to perform exorcisms and he'll tell you it's everywhere: that's why three times a week he finds his podgy fingers gripping the heads of the lost, sad and mad, demanding they 'Renounce The Devil!' in whiplashing spasms. And maybe he's right. Maybe hell is to be alive in Britain in January 1974. Government instructions to save energy by boiling everything in one pan, by stopping ironing knickers, by foregoing the bourgeois luxury of electric blankets. A country so depressed by want of light and heat and hope it gets its kicks watching the starving inmates of *Colditz* in the sacred hour before the telly shuts down again. Oh, it's hell, all right. Just switch on the radio. There's Cozy Powell and his 'Dance With The Devil' paradiddling up the charts. Give it a few weeks and the woman who played bass on it will leapfrog him with her own 'Devil Gate Drive'. It's as the vicar from Chalk Farm fears. 'Some people do not want the evil spirits to leave them.' Hell is anywhere on Earth there's sympathy for The Devil.

Even Barnes. Where Mick recorded 'Sympathy For The Devil' and the walls of Olympic haven't much changed in the five-and-a-half years since. The panels and screens are still mustard and orange, the square carpet tiles are still grey and the engineers still smell of extended lunch hours in the Red Lion. Only now there's two studios. The one the Stones used and this newer one, Studio 2, where Mick perches on a plastic hourglass stool in the corner, lips puckering inquisitively as he watches David as a mother might her child playing in a sandpit: cross-legged on the ground surrounded by paper and pens among jack leads wriggling across the floor from one distant socket to another like tributaries of the Amazon basin; between his knees, the hardback 1974 desk diary he uses as a board to slice a handwritten sheet into strips, line by line, using a metal ruler and scalpel.

'Cut-ups,' he tells Mick. An old Dadaist trick he's borrowed from his pal 'Bill' Burroughs. You chop up existing phrases or sentences, then mix the different pieces at random to create abstract new meanings. It's how Bill writes his novels and it's how David's been trying to write lyrics for the songs he's been recording here since Christmas, not that anyone would guess. On first listen they sound reassuringly David, some reassuringly Ziggy, ever grander in their starry romanticism, ever tougher in their street punk rock'n'roll.

Like the one he's just played for Mick. Took him some nerve too. David calls it 'Rebel Rebel', but Mick knows it by another name, and he should. He's the one who wrote it with Keith Richards in 1965. Its tempo, its chords, its twang, its neon-bathed stilettos clacking down a concrete catwalk are the same as '(I Can't Get No) Satisfaction'. But now he sees David with his razor, Mick understands. He's just sliced up and rejiggled the notes of Keith's riff, same as he's doing with those scraps of paper. 'Rebel Rebel' is 'Satisfaction' Burroughsed. One artist making a naked lunch out of another's beggar's banquet.

Mick doesn't mind. As he always says, 'It's only rock'n'roll, man, so what the hell?' It's all harmless flattery. Three-and-a-half years older than David, he's become something like a big brother to him, the wise old 'grandfather of pop' there to answer his every question. About money, about the business, about managers, about investments, about staying sane and staying on top. 'You spend an awful lot of time at home with your old lady,' says Mick, who thinks he needs to jet away more often, as he does, chasing the next test match to Trinidad, or tanning his skinny *Lord of the Flies* physique on the patio of Princess Margaret's £400-a-week villa in the Caribbean. 'Don't hang around with your family more than you have to, man. Me, I'm not the least bit domesticated.'

And just like any hero-worshipping kid brother, David's always paying gumshoe attention to everything Mick says, does or buys. The loafers he wears, the records he plays, the books he reads, the restaurants where he eats. Like the other day when the Bowies popped round Cheyne Walk for dinner with him and his own old lady, Bianca. The gals spent the night screeching gossip and gowns while the boys pored over some funky new fantasy paintings of the Stones Mick showed him created by a Belgian artist for a forthcoming book. David wouldn't leave the subject alone. *Who* was this Guy Peellaert? *Where* was his studio? *Where* could he buy his work? Only when Mick told him he was based in Paris and designing the cover of the next Stones album did the grilling stop. When David, falling quiet, slumped back sipping his vodka with ever so strange a leer on his face.

A bit like the one he's got now, sat there slicing on the studio floor in his blue cloche hat and tatty green pullover. The tenth worst-dressed woman of 1973. While Mick in his yellow Oxford bags and loose cotton jacket is already in the running against Captain Mark Phillips for 1974's International Male Elegance Award. But then he can only help David so much. Listen to him air all his inner fears and private hauntings. Give him what advice he thinks he needs. Recommend the odd Gore Vidal book. Tell him not to work so hard. Swap the occasional lover. Steal his make-up artist. Take the piss out of his trousers. Everything else going on beneath that cloche hat is David's own business. Well, look at him – just voted *Disc* magazine's 'Top Male Vocalist', British *and* International, yet here he is in a raggedy granny jumper playing with strips of paper like he's Susan Stranks.

Mick pouts a stifled laugh and shakes his head.

Man! What the bloody hell does he think he's doing?

HE DOESN'T KNOW. That's the beauty of cut-ups. You never do. You write, you chop, you scramble, you read, you decode. For David, it's less about atom-smashing syntax than a form of psychic divination, a bit like tarot cards. Chance words come together and mysteries reveal themselves. Home truths. Past secrets. Future legends.

With every drag of the scalpel he severs himself from the dying fictions still bearing his name in this week's papers. Yesterday's doomed hopes, now today's threadbare lies. His West End musical of George Orwell's *Nineteen Eighty-Four*. His Broadway revue *The Ziggy Stardust Show*. His sequel covers album, the one he referred to as '*Pin Ups 2*'. All ancient histories discarded in the time it takes to shred one foolscap sheet into so much spaghetti. Cut up. Rearrange. Start again.

The songs that remain are now amputated body parts he must stitch together to make a brand-new monster. One no longer beholden to any fate once in store for Winston Smith or Ziggy Stardust, where the former's 'We Are The Dead' can conjoin with the latter's 'Rock 'N' Roll With Me' leaving no visible scars. The failure to finish either musical all the way to a theatrical run becomes an unseen liberation. The only performance David now need worry about is the two-act play at 33⅓ rpm. The only leading role, himself. And while much of the scenery is still recognisably Suffragette City or Airstrip One, the libretto constantly changes according to whatever mental plagues possess him on any given day.

It could be Fritz Lang's *Metropolis*, part of the Hampstead Everyman's 'Classics of the German Cinema' season which he's taken to see the week after his 27th birthday, its Cubist sci-fi cityscapes, mad inventors, robot women and workers sacrificing themselves to the demon Moloch of industry etched so deep upon his eyeballs that every time he shuts their lids he can rewatch it like a flicker book. It could be Bill's most recent novel *The Wild Boys* and its tribal gangs of '*glider boys with bows and laser guns, roller-skate boys, blue jockstraps and steel helmets, eighteen inch bowie knives*'. It could be a late night visit from Rod Stewart and Ronnie Wood, arms rattling with Liebfraumilch and an advance copy of the Faces' live LP *Coast To Coast: Overture And Beginners*. It could be looking up from his paper play one day to find Pete Townshend staring back at him, beak squashed up against the control-room glass wondering what the *Tommy* David's up to with all his high-concept artyfartying. It could be the Broadway melody of Rodgers and Hart's 'Bewitched, Bothered And Bewildered'. It could be the saxophone Angie bought him for Christmas. It could be a sudden desire to change all the bulbs in the studio to red. It could be Mick laughing his usual 'man, it's only rock'n'roll'. It could be swastika nightmares of genocide.

David can do anything he wants because there's no one to stop him. He employs a tiny handful of musicians who come in only when he needs them to play only what he tells them. Most of the instruments he plays himself – as he brags to Mick, 'pretty well everything except piano and drums' – and for the first time in eight albums he is his own producer, with no one to answer to other than his ego. And his ego, cornfed on sex and powdered plant toxins, is David Bowie's biggest fan.

And why shouldn't it be? Just listen to him *sing*.

There are people who cannot sing and when they try it's as ugly as a rye-blind bum seeing how many parked cars they can bounce off till they crack their head on the kerb. There are those who *think* they can sing, deaf to their zombie-footed stiffness of patients dragging drips on castors. There are singers who plod, singers who stroll, singers who skip and singers who run. And there are those, not many, David being one of the chosen few, who dance. Not just any old ballroom foxtrotter or nightclub jiver, but a *dancer*. A Nijinsky, an Astaire. The sort of dancing that obeys its own gravity so they hang in the air longer than you think humanly possible, like there's no crouching depths they can't spring from and no cloudless heights they can't spring to, their muscles moving as if in weightless slow motion, leaping strong as skyrockets, landing soft as feathers. This is how David sings. He has never not been able to sing, and he has never not sung well, but on these new songs he sings in arabesques and somersaults. Like a singer who wishes to be remembered and knows precisely when his voice is too beautiful to forget. Because if immortality was ever his goal, on these songs he signs his insurance policy.

As David's Orwell album is rubbed out by his Ziggy album, is redrawn by his *Wild Boys* album, is crosshatched by his *Metropolis* album, he takes a last step back to try and make sense of what it all *means*. But there's what he sings and what he says, and when the two join together they, too, might as well be random cut-ups.

He sings about a post-apocalyptic dystopia, then says it's 'a backward look at the Sixties and Seventies'.

He sings about sex in doorways and taking drugs, then says it's 'a very political album'.

He sings about deformity and Tod Browning's *Freaks*, then says it's 'my protest'.

He sings of feeling scared and lonely, then says 'this album is more me than anything I've done previously'.

Unless it's true? David, secretly a little scared and perhaps genuinely lonely, whether he's here with Mick or Bill or the studio ghost of Jimi Hendrix. Where time is not made of minutes but ticking white lines: paper strips, powder sniffs, mini-Moog keys and the barrels of Gitanes. Living like a bat between dusk and dawn, never seeing sunlight but for the few footsteps between home and car then car and studio. Perfectly isolated from the blacked-out hungry city around him, barricaded in his fortress against the armies of diseased mutants crawling out there in the darkness. As the lights flicker, and the pipes gurgle, and the radiators turn deathly cold. Just like every other place that isn't heaven.

FOUR

THEY CALL IT 'BROWN SUGAR'. How come it tastes so good? Because it's 33 per cent heroin, 60 per cent caffeine and 7 per cent morphine. It looks like demerara too, which is how Chinese smugglers are shipping it into Britain in plastic sacks. Sweet and deadly. One fix could kill anyone, and there's already too many anyones with arms like cribbage boards crowding the London morgues. The Yard have been trying to clean up the streets as best they can with a lengthy undercover op in Chinatown where it takes one WPC 'disguised' in jeans and plimsolls to smash the racket of a Soho croupier named Ping Fook Fung. They offer him a reduced sentence if he'll turn rat and tell them how he sneaks it in all the way from the Far East. Fung laughs and runs a finger across his throat. 'Me live, not dead.' And goes down for nine years.

But there are far too many poppies, way too many Chinamen and not nearly enough bobbies as dedicated as WPC 161. The filthy powder still blows up and down Gerrard Street like a dune in a sandstorm. A hitch hike to heaven for £7 a time and hell knows in a few hours they'll be back for another. And another. And another.

In this discontented winter of Fairy-soft hands and 'Tiger Feet', the only sure way to see a Chinese opium lord served tough justice is to walk a little further down to Leicester Square where a crime boss named Han gets his four times a day in the Warner West End. There's no shortage of takers and haven't been since *Enter the Dragon* opened in January. When its star, Bruce Lee, died suddenly of a brain aneurysm last summer aged 32 it didn't even make the Stop Press. Now, literally overnight, he's as big as Elvis, cooler than Clint Eastwood and more mourned than James Dean. If one of his 'Chop Suey Westerns' isn't enough you can always gorge on *Fist of Fury* round the corner at the Oscar or *The Big Boss* at Odeons around the capital. Two sisters from the East End have, each over a dozen times, both so convinced their nunchucking heartthrob must still be alive and hiding in secret they're prepared to save £15 a week from their secretarial jobs to fund a Lee-finding pilgrimage to Hong Kong. At which rate they'll be boarding their plane some time round about October 1977.

Lee, the fastest-selling poster offer in *The Sun* since Little Jimmy Osmond, is only half the reason there are playgrounds running amok with kids as young as five scissor-kicking their way to spinal paralysis. The other is Caine, the Shaolin cowboy of *Kung Fu*, airing on different days in different ITV regions, all far too early for those like the *Evening Standard* who find its popularity '*profoundly disquieting*'. So does Caine himself, hippie actor David Carradine, who never watches it because he doesn't own a TV set, just a home in Laurel Canyon with a leaky roof and a car with one working headlight and a fender held together by string. He says the hit series has made him 'more bread than I know what to do with', a problem the many dealers of Los Angeles are trying their very hardest to help him solve. But whether he likes it or not, *Kung Fu*'s made him a teenage pin-up: as of next month it'll even have its own comic strip in *Look-In*. And so long as he is, and it does, and so long as kids are too busy chopping the air above the settee in screaming 'HI-YA!'s to heed the pre-show warning 'if practised by the untrained it could be dangerous', so the chances of a 9-year-old boy from Finsbury Park taking a flying kick at some gym apparatus only to break his skull remain tragically high.

Questions about the crisis of kung fu Britain have yet to be asked in parliament, but then this very week parliament has just been dissolved. After months of union pressure and brassnecked denial, Heath has finally 'named the day', and on February 28th he's confident that day, and its next majority government, will be his. The choice is more or less the same as it was four years ago. Him or Harold Wilson, or the rank outside coalition threat of Rod Stewart's man, the Liberals' Jeremy Thorpe.

Early polls tell Heath he'll scrape it, so it's with a blind faith and a hearty appetite that he spends his first Sunday evening since calling the election dining with friends at his favourite Knightsbridge restaurant, Mr Chow. Between them they polish off spare ribs, stewed dumplings, prawns, crab, chicken, sweet and sour pork, an entire Peking duck and a sackful of boiled rice. His final bill comes to fifty pounds – almost double what the average miner he accuses of holding the country to ransom earns in a week. For the same price he could buy around seven fixes of Ping Fook Fung's heroin. But in this Chinese New Year of the Tiger, as Mud won't let us forget, you pays your yen, you takes your choice.

'BLOW'. DAVID'S CHOICE. Fifty quid gets him two grams and two grams is not nearly enough to see him through a five-hour musical gala in a Dutch exhibition centre wondering how best to excuse himself to the nearest bathroom without being seen by cameras broadcasting to the biggest live audience in Western Europe after the Eurovision Song Contest.

'Is that YOU?'

A stupid question. Who else could it be? Sat next to Angie – herself unmistakably blonde machine-gun-eyed Angie – in the second row with his red cockatoo hair and half-mast dungarees, a spotted neckerchief, a hoop earring, knee-length boots and a pirate patch over his right eye.

'Is that really YOU?'

Conspicuously so. Even with that eyepatch, making fashion out of affliction, covering up the nasty dose of conjunctivitis he picked up somewhere between home, Harwich and the Amstel Hotel.

'Is that David?'

It is. Here in Amsterdam where he's been lured under the pretence of accepting an award. These days he gets them all the time from the UK music papers, usually sending surrogates to pick up on his behalf, but an Edison, the Dutch equivalent of a Grammy, is deemed prestigious enough to collect in person, which he did, at a reception lunch two days ago. In between he's made time to fiddle with his album in a local studio and mime 'Rebel Rebel' for a Dutch TV show. But other than polite obligation there is no earthly reason for him also to be here in attendance at the Grand Gala du Disque.

'A fantastic star!'

One completely out of place among the cinched dresses and cummerbunds, the cufflinks and the strings of pearls, the balding executives and their mistress-blind wives, the idle programme flicking and the automatic applause for all this whitey-white rollmop music for whitey-white rollmop people.

'DAVID BOOEE!'

The wrong syllable booms from the stage, inches from where David sits pretending not to be here, where a man in a velvet tux and a dickie bow is doing his best to draw the attention of everyone in the auditorium to the fact David actually is.

'BOWIE!'

Tony Orlando, the man in the tux, corrects himself. The audience applaud. Then, as he resumes the song he interrupted in order to alert both the crowd and the viewers at home to the presence of the fantastic star whose surname he struggles to pronounce, Orlando winks at Angie.

'See if he sings along with me.'

The song is 'Tie A Yellow Ribbon Round The Ole Oak Tree'.

David's lips do not move.

THEY DON'T HAVE TO. Not for Angie to know what he's thinking. She always knows, like she can hear his thoughts dot-dot-dashing through the airwaves in morse code. She knows when he's agitated, like just then, squirming in the spotlight of Orlando and his cruise-ship wisecracks, or bored, like right now, itching to up his grammage the first chance he gets. Whatever he's thinking, Angie hears, loud and clear. When he's being too slow making up his mind, like the house they saw in Holland Park which he still can't decide whether to buy or not. When not to disturb him when he's lost in his music on the far side of their living room, a man in a cross-legged trance bent over a synthesizer like the Phantom of the Opera. When not to ask where he's been when he slumps home spent-eyed, stinking of someone else's sweat, and instinct tells her she probably wouldn't like the answer. That's the secret to any successful open marriage. Self-deceit and selective information. But she always knows. Same as the second a black female trio walk out on the gala stage she knows he wants to fuck the lot of them.

Smooth sexy brown skin like theirs? Oh, her David can't get enough of it. Like Ava, the black lover he picked up like a holiday souvenir on his last world tour, the one who's just gone and upped back to America thanks to the hints Angie dropped subtle as anvils off a cliff in a Road Runner cartoon. Oh, she knows! Watching them shimmy and twirl singing 'Dirty Old Man', she can hear his dirty young brain flicker like a stag film, goggling at their hips pivoting and dipping, his eyes eating them up one by one, his groin tensing, his back bristling at the prospect of their shiny nails dragging down his shoulder blades hard as a garden rake. Of course, she knows! Right now he's thinking about pounding all three of them in the same bed, at the same time, and the funny thing is she can't even blame him. Hell, they're making her feel pretty horny herself. Well, look at them, with their sashaying limbs and their glittery frocks and all that sensual *hoo-ooh! hah-aah!* moaning. Oh, Angie knows because – surely? – anyone here can see. THESE GALS ARE *FAAABULOUS* . . .

THEY ARE. The Three Degrees, Philadelphia's fabulous answer to the Supremes, or as their manager would have it, a supreme Supremes 'with three Diana Rosses instead of one'. By name, Fay, Valerie and Sheila, a diamond-tonsilled trio with more glamour than class, more class than sex and more sex than style. *Of course* David wants to fuck them, but only through force of habit. Most normal people run on food and sleep. David used to, briefly, when he was a little more like a normal person, but now he isn't. Now he is David Bowie 'fantastic star'. Now he runs on sex and drugs. Show him a gram and he'll want it up his nose. Show him a beautiful black woman and he'll want her in his bed. But though Angie isn't wrong, because Angie rarely is, kneejerk lust is only half the story of the chemical explosion happening right now between David's ears.

It's the music. Their music. The sweet harmonies and all that *hoo-ooh! hah-aah!* Even though their usual fluid groove is stymied by the lumpy live gala orchestra – forty-five musicians white as raw turnips conducted by a man named Harry van Hoof – the silvery sound of the Three Degrees still lights up David's head like a burning bush, a calling from three ebony archangels to follow this vibration to its celestial source.

Is this the beginning?

He'd better believe it. Wound up tight as he is, he knows none of this is the fine grit dissolving on his mucous membrane. Because even while he subsists on his daily staples of sex and drugs, David still lives for music. And he wants theirs.

'May god love ya! We sho' do!'

He wants it even more once they swish off stage and the whitey-white curds-and-whey cabaret returns in a vengeance of beards and guitars and more teeth and tuxedos. Feels it like a physical burning agony. A cockroaches-crawling-under-his-skin withdrawal. A literal soul cold turkey.

And then along comes Christmas dinner.

In the shape of a man who looks like he's eaten the Christmas dinner of every member of the orchestra. Forty-five plates of meat 'n' gravy and all the trimmings. With extra stuffing.

'Mmm-mmm.'

He even speaks like a man who's just polished off forty-five Christmas dinners. A deep, satisfied rumble smacking its lips somewhere around his lower intestines, but not so satisfied it couldn't sneak in another portion. It's a voice of endless appetite, of unquenchable desire, of 'uh-huh', 'right on', 'oh baby' and 'mmm-mmm'.

And nobody 'uh-huh's, 'right on's, 'oh baby's and 'mmm-mmm's like Barry White.

When Barry sings you can hear God orgasm. And, as he only knows, God orgasms very, very, very, very, very, very slowly. Almost as slowly as Barry moves. He doesn't, much, whether stood behind the mic or sat at his piano. But then he doesn't have to. The motion is all in the music. A rippling tidal wave of unzipping sensuality, cresting through long verses of button-popping dramatic tension, crashing in syrupy choruses foaming with romantic ecstasy. Just a few bars of 'Never, Never Gonna Give Ya Up' and the whole place is drenched. Ruddy-cheeked women cross and uncross their legs, bowties are loosened and wingtips tremble. And in Row B, an eyepatch gyrates to the bob of its redheaded host in time to the sheet-grinding rhythm.

Which is when David knows that he finally *knows*, so close to Barry he can see the sweat bubbling down his cheeks like cooking juices. Knows what he already knew watching the Three Degrees, but listening to Barry removes any last doubt. Knows even though he has his post-nuclear sci-fi album still to finish and a new single, out today, that sounds much too much like an old single by the Rolling Stones. Knows even as last year's haircut prickles his neck like a jailer's key fob to the prison of Ziggy Stardust. Knows that all *that* is all over. Finally knows what he wants and it's not rock'n'roll but *hoo-ooh! hah-aah!* and *ooh, what a groove.* Finally knows who he is and it's not who his loyal subjects back in Bowietannia think.

'Is that YOU?'

Oh, go on, Orlando. Ask him again.

'Is that really YOU?'

Not anymore, suckers. David's a soul man.

YOU WOULDN'T NOTICE HER. Not straight away. Discreet as a shadowy film extra in her curly brown hair and plain sleeveless dress, sat on the aisle nearest the stage, two seats from David, separated only by Angie.

Someone from Mainman had to accompany the Bowies to Amsterdam, and as Defries was too tied up in New York she was the London office's obvious choice. Obvious since she as good as runs the London office these days and quite obviously chose herself. Defries green-lighted all travel expenses without hesitation. Corinne has yet to let him down.

The short interval over, faces powdered and noses pinched, the second half of the never-ending Grand Gala du Disque opens with the Carpenters. Centre stage, bare-armed and smiling in a pale blue smock, Karen coos of longing to be close to someone. For now, two seats from David is close enough for Corinne. To feel the vibration in her seatback when he rocks his body to the Three Degrees. To feel Angie between them like an electric fence. To never fully lose sight of him from the furthest corner of her right eye, even as she feigns interest in Karen, now changing her tune to the one about the love she's found ever since he's been around that's put her on top of the world.

Two seats from David, a heart quietly thumps.

FIVE

TOP OF THE WORLD and top of the charts. In a bleak British winter of rainy days and Mondays, soppy British ears take shelter beneath the Carpenters. Their chocolate-brown *Singles* collection has been number 1 since the beginning of February and would have been there sooner if it weren't delayed by the three-day week pressing-plant crisis. At 45 rpm, the teens are still rampaging to the dying bumps of glam's dodgems from The Sweet, Suzi and Mud. But at 33⅓, rock'n'roll is dead. Long live shoo-be-doo-lang-lang.

Exactly one week after the Grand Gala du Disque, Karen and her brother Richard have touts' pockets bulging outside London's Royal Festival Hall where tickets are swapping for over three times face value. It'll be the same tomorrow when they move to the Hammersmith Odeon, and on Sunday when they play two shows at the Talk of the Town where they'll still be shoo-be-doo-lang-langing at 3 a.m. 'No, it's not rock,' states Richard, who's since made front-page headlines of *Melody Maker* after calling the New York Dolls 'a bunch of amateurs'. His little sister says the same about Mott The Hoople. '*Awful*. Screaming at the top of their lungs.'

So what about David Bowie?

'I liked "Space Oddity",' admits Richard, 'but no, I wouldn't go out and buy one of his albums.'

Four miles north from the rockless Festival Hall, as Karen *sha-la-la-la-las* and Richard *woah-oh-oh-ohs*, a very different capacity crowd, who anyone would safely bet all must have bought at least one David Bowie album, fix their eyes on the still-empty stage of the Rainbow. Because it's their hope, and their hunch, that by the time they file out into the chilly Finsbury Park night, David Bowie will have been on it. It's not his name on the ticket, nor the outside marquee, nor the fan club stall in the foyer, nor its posters and T-shirts on sale, nor the green arm bands of the road crew scurrying in the wings. But, as Defries knows, you don't have to sell Bowie to sell Bowie. Just look at this week's Top 10. There he is at number 3 with 'The Man Who Sold The World'. Not Bowie in body but Bowie in demonic form possessing Lulu, a woman who still earns a crust as the wifey face of Freemans catalogue, now popping up on telly doing his androgynous bidding in a suit and fedora like a munchkin mobster. The same goes for tonight, the first of two sell-out shows at the Rainbow. Everyone here to see David Bowie. Everyone here with a ticket for Mick Ronson.

Nothing ever being true until it's officially denied, Mainman have issued a press statement making it clear: '*David Bowie will not be appearing with Mick Ronson at the Rainbow*'.

The 3,000 disciples here tonight of course know better. You can hear it with every breath they exhale.

Bowie is here! Bowie is here!
Somewhere.
Bowie is here! Bowie is here!
They can feel him.
Bowie is here! Bowie is here!
Smell him.
Bowie is here! Bowie is here!
SEE HIM!
Sitting in the balcony, next to Angie, clear as if they were waxworks in Madame Tussauds. Him with his shaved eyebrows, bony cheeks and shock of red hair. Her with her pale complexion, bottle blonde and bright lipstick.

'OHMYGOD!'
Two girls scuttle like shore crabs over the backs of seats until they collapse in the row behind him, pen and paper trembling.

'*David!*' squeaks the bustier blonde one with thick green eyeshadow. 'P-p-please give us your autograph?'

He twists round, blinking at her pen. 'I'm not 'im,' he sniffs. Then twists back.

The blonde shakes in confusion. 'Wot?'

'I'm not 'im.'

She frowns. 'Aw, please!'

Her friend with curly brown hair and a sequined top leans over and mutters in her ear. The blonde smiles and nods.

'Go on, David! She says you are too!'

'I'm not. I just look like 'im.'

'Oh, stop messing! Why you sat with Angie then?'

'That's not 'er.'

'It bloody is!'

A tug at her sleeve from her curly friend. 'Come on, Brend. Maybe we should go?'

Except they can't. They're hemmed in either side by a skinny boy in denims with a dangly earring and a girl with spiky hair and a lightning flash on her face. More pens. More pleading.

'*DAVID!*'

'Look!' he laughs. 'I told ya. I'm not 'im!'

He's right. He's not 'im. And that's not 'er either.

His name is Henry, not David, and that's Lesley, not Angie, and she's his girlfriend, not his wife. Henry is 19 years old, and for the last two of those he's been a work-in-progress human chrysalis doing everything in his cosmetic power to transform himself into David's replica. He's a commercial artist by day and sometime singer with a band called Bearded Ladies by night, and though he might sound it when repeating 'I'm not 'im' like a Cockney parrot, Henry is not daft. He's been chased down streets, had strangers molest him shoving phone numbers in his pockets and the clothes Lesley's mother makes for him torn from his 28-inch waist. He knows exactly what he's doing here, blatantly Bowieing in the balcony with his Angie-a-like bird, surrounded by fans all as dotty as he is about the prospect of seeing the real thing on stage tonight.

'I'm not 'im,' he repeats.

But the fans won't hear it. 'Oh, go on!'

Henry smirks. A gawky chancer's smirk that shatters any illusion he might really be David Bowie. But it doesn't stop them and it doesn't stop him. He proudly seizes the nearest pen and signs in looping script –

David Bowie

They knew it!
BOWIE IS HERE! BOWIE IS HERE! BOWIE IS HERE!
Yes. Bowie is here. But not sitting in the balcony. Not anywhere any of the crowd can see or pester him. Hidden from view, up at the very back in what used to be the projection room when the Rainbow was a cinema. Safe behind glass, eyes alert and sinuses crackling, peeking out with a perfect view of the stage. That's 'im.

And there, next to him, in a Cuban cloud of hype and hubris, is Defries. He flew in from New York this morning to be here. That's how important this is. So important he's paid for a Mainman film crew to capture what he knows will be a piece of history: the unveiling of his new model Bowie Mk II.

It's been Defries's brainwave to launch Ronson from his first curtain-up as a ready-made superstar. Not with cautious low-key club shows out of town to iron out any creases and overcome any butterflies but here at the Rainbow, starting as he means him to go on, selling out two nights at the same venue Stevie Wonder sold out only a few weeks ago. Proving it doesn't matter the audience won't have heard a note of Mick's debut album, *Slaughter On 10th Avenue*, which should've been out by now except UK manufacturing delays have forced the label to start pressing and shipping it over late from America. Or that his debut single, a cover of Elvis Presley's 'Love Me Tender', is so bad that when he plays it this evening someone cries 'Murder!' What matters is media hoopla and a full house. What matters is selling Bowie even when it isn't Bowie.

Tonight, it definitely isn't. It's a first-night-nervous-wreck of a guitar player from Hull in a stripey gondolier top and knotted neckerchief, cattle-prodded into the spotlight where the stress of having to learn his lines and not bump into the furniture is there for all to see. That furniture being a band including David's pianist Mike Garson dressed in white tails, fellow ex-Spider From Mars Trevor on bass, David's trusted Beckenham neighbour Mark Pritchett on rhythm, the female backing trio Thunderthighs who sang the *doot-doot-doots* on 'Walk On The Wild Side', a five-man horn section and a partially employed so therefore rather bored-looking 19-piece orchestra. Not one of whom can save him.

'PLAY US A BOWIE SONG!'

It takes a while before the heckles come. But when they do, they form battalions.

'WHERE'S DAVID?'

He's in the projection room, watching the money he's earned for Mainman pouring down the drain of Defries's doomed *Star is Born* fantasy. The one starring Mick Ronson called *Slaughter on the Seven Sisters Road*. Wishing he was watching the Three Degrees instead as he stubs out a Gitane and pulls another from its packet, balancing it between his lips and fumbling in his pocket for a lighter. Finding one, he brings it up to his chin.

KRRRANG-GU-GANG!

And freezes.

KRRRANG-GU-GANG!

The crowd is screaming to a familiar chord.

KRRRANG-GU-GANG!

David grips his lighter, unable to click a flame.

KRRRANG-GU-GANG!

No . . . Surely? thinks David. *He wouldn't?*

And then Mick sings.

'Am an alley-gay-tah!'

Yes. He fucking would.

On stage, legs apart, guitar aloft like a standard bearer, the audience berserk and rushing towards him, Mick Ronson is singing 'Moonage Daydream' by David Bowie. The song he played on and helped arrange and has performed maybe a hundred times with David in the past. But never, until tonight, has he played it without David. Played it instead of David. Played it to a packed house willing to suspend disbelief they're watching David. Played it like he *is* David.

In the projection room, the real David Bowie clicks a flame. He takes a hard deep drag as if trying to suck the nicotine in a single go like poison from a snake bite. He pulls it from his mouth. He clenches his teeth. He takes another fierce puff and says something under his breath.

Something that sounded a lot like 'cunt'.

ACROSS TOWN ON THE SOUTHBANK, Karen and Richard – having me-oh-my-ohed, da-doo-ron-ronned, shing-a-ling-a-linged and only just begun – are taking their final bows. With two more shows tomorrow, they'll soon be safely tucked up in their separate fluffy five-star beds by 1 a.m.

Around the time the Ronson afterparty at Blake's Hotel in South Kensington is in full damage-limitation swing. Defries is here, of course, but for reasons nobody's told, David isn't. A shame, and something of a mystery since he only lives round the corner. But at least Mick, the man of the hour, is. And so, to his amazement, is young Henry.

The Mainman staff spotted him in the foyer being manhandled by fans and helped bundle him out of a side entrance for his own safety. They can't get over his likeness either, so uncanny, they say, he might come in handy in the future as an official decoy when trying to sneak David in and out of venues. Which is why, as an acid test, they bring him and his girlfriend Lesley along to Blake's on Roland Gardens where he's introduced to the man of the hour. Even Ronson agrees he's a dead ringer for his old boss.

'Wow!' he laughs. 'I'm going to have to start calling you David.'

Henry blushes as they ceremonially clink glasses. The crisp bell-like sound of one David Bowie impersonator congratulating another.

SUNRISE OVER SOUTH KENSINGTON. The party is over in Blake's Hotel. The glasses collected, the ashtrays emptied and all imposters gone to their beds. But sure as the Earth spins, night will fall again. And when it falls, the darkness drops like a bomb.

A week passes, and on Roland Gardens, only a few doors down from Blake's, a doorbell rings. It's answered by a young woman called Jan, not long home alone from her shift at Buckingham Palace where she answers correspondence for Princess Anne. On the doorstep are two men she presumes are friends of her two flatmates. She invites them inside to wait. Fifteen minutes later she's tied to a bed, having been stripped and raped at knifepoint. A similar fate awaits another flatmate who comes home too soon while the apartment is still being ransacked. Both girls are eventually left trussed up together, terrified and naked on the bedroom floor.

As they shiver and wait to be discovered, two miles away in Downing Street Edward Heath is quite evidently mistaken in thinking nobody is having as bad a day as he is.

Yesterday, the nation decided. Yesterday, the *Mail* confidently predicted 'A HANDSOME WIN FOR HEATH'. Yesterday, millions of voters braced wintry showers to their nearest polling station to grip a pencil on a piece of string, having already made up their minds: about the three-day week, about the railways, about the fact a packet of Dreft washing powder is nearly twice the price it was when Heath got into power four years ago. Yesterday, before the polls had closed the bookies had to shorten the odds on Labour to avoid a bankrupting payout. Yesterday, Heath was still Prime Minister and contemplating his next slap-up celebration at Mr Chow's.

Today, Heath has just returned from the Palace – where the royal secretary still hogtied naked in Roland Gardens had been working hours earlier – to tell Her Majesty that despite a devastating outcome for his Tories, resulting in shock Labour gains and a deadlocked government with no outright majority, he has no intention of resigning. Tonight he will sleep very badly, if at all, and spend the weekend bravefacing, denying, plotting and begging Jeremy Thorpe to form a Tory–Liberal coalition. The two party leaders meet on Saturday afternoon and again on Sunday evening. But by the time the next episode of *Colditz* airs on Monday night, it's Labour's Harold Wilson who'll be declared PM. 'I have nothing to say but my prayers,' pipes Harold as the Number 10 removal men gather the last of his predecessor's artefacts: some yachting medals, sheet music, an anorak, a jar of instant coffee and a cheese grater. Before the first week of his new premiership is through, Wilson will settle with the miners and end the three-day week. In tandem the rains cease, the buds blossom and March begins so dry and mild that a craze originating in America becomes a national epidemic keeping magistrates' courts busy in fines averaging £20 a streak. As one defendant explains, they do it 'to liven things up, because everything has been so grim in the last few months'. At number 3 The Hollies are singing 'The Air That I Breathe' and already that of Wilson's Britain – where hairy men and

buxom women sprint naked through pubs, parks and train platforms –
tastes a little less stale.

THE NEAREST POLLING STATION to David was the Chenil Galleries on
the King's Road. So close he could have popped there and back from his
Oakley Street home in under ten minutes. Except he didn't.

He spent most of that day in the same place he spends most of this one.
The ground floor of a terraced house midway between Shepherd's Bush
and Hammersmith, just a few doors up from a similar bayfront home
where the director of the new *Three Musketeers* film, Richard Lester,
shot scenes for his Sixties comedy *The Knack . . . and How to Get It*.
Separating that house from his is a block of flats filling the hole left when
the Luftwaffe took care of the original numbers 2 to 6 Melrose Terrace.
But today, like election day, all is eerily calm. No bombs, no streakers, no
breeze and, even if there were, no leaves to rustle on the lime tree outside
number 9. But behind its door, the sound of the end of the world.

The sound has a name. *Diamond Dogs.* The title of the album David
has finished recording but still needs to mix, which brings him here to
the new home studio of his old friend Tony Visconti. So new you can
still smell the sawdust in the air from Tony's carpentry. The rest of the
house is unoccupied, waiting for him and his wife Mary and their baby
son to move in from their flat in Putney. Until they do it's just a bare
squatter-ready shell save the downstairs homemade bunker, big enough
for a 16-track desk and two Habitat chairs supplied by David in the
absence of any furniture. Their only disturbance is the nightly ring of
the doorbell by a restaurant courier delivering fine claret and hot steak
dinners. Everything else is work and cigarettes.

He can trust Tony. Trust him as he can't any other Tony in his life.
It's been four years since they last worked together, but once the tapes
roll their lives splice so neatly back together even they can't see the join.
He also needs him, as a rally driver needs a good mechanic. It's David's
hands on the wheel but it's Tony's eye on the pressure gauge; David who
knows where he's going, Tony who knows how to cut the corners. Other
than assisting with the mix, just as Paul McCartney turned to Tony to
orchestrate his latest, *Band On The Run*, so David asks if he'll wrap strings

around '1984'. Which he does, tying it in such soulful bows he makes it sound as David always hoped it would sound. Black and American.

The rest of it sounds white and dystopian. Post-nuclear, post-civilisation, post-glam and post-rock'n'roll. The pop equivalent of a Seventies science-fiction film, and like every major science-fiction film so far this decade, *Diamond Dogs* is a future nightmare. The Seventies knows no other kind. Whenever cinema looks into its crystal ball these days it sees only darkness. The droogie street violence of *A Clockwork Orange*. The zombie pandemic of *The Omega Man*. The ecological apocalypse of *Silent Running*. The state cannibalism of *Soylent Green*. The sex fascism of *THX 1138*. And still the terrors keep on coming. Two more open in London this month: the psychopathic android drama *Westworld* and the cursed immortality fable *Zardoz* starring Sean Connery as a twenty-third-century pigtailed pagan savage in kinky boots and a red jockstrap. Its poster tagline is 'BEYOND 1984, BEYOND 2001'. The sound of *Diamond Dogs* defined.

Day after day in Melrose Terrace, David knits and Tony knots, cutting out and stitching in, weaving intros over outros, warping songs in and out of one another, the mixing desk their sonic loom. It sounds nothing like David's ever made before since all he's ever made before is albums full of songs. This one isn't. From its opening mutant wolf howl to the final looping '*bruh*' of '*brother*', blasted by Tony's new digital delay gizmo making it stutter like a malfunctioning Dalek, though storyless it is still one long continuous scenario demanding to be heard in sequence. Never has David made a record pulled together from so much disparate bric-a-brac. Never has he made a record sounding so complete. As an album, as a singular creation, as a work of art, as a warp factor leap for Seventies rock'n'roll, as its necessary assassin and its year-zero restart, as the last dance on glam's grave, as pop's evolutionary shortcut to the Eighties, as a dead heat between vibes versus intellect, as a mockery of his peers and a catastrophe for his rivals, as the real masterpiece to knock *Aladdin* and *Ziggy* into silver and bronze, as the removal of any last shred of critical doubt, as a record that looks The Devil in the eye and laughs 'bet even *you* wish you were David Bowie', *Diamond Dogs* is . . .

'*Ow-oooooooo!*'

. . . perfect.

★

OUTSIDE MELROSE TERRACE, life is less so. As the factory toots in the old five-day week, as the TV closedown returns to the right side of midnight, as women in wet T-shirts boost sales of Manikin cigars, as one processed din from ChinniChapp replaces another at number 1, David's new single hits the post at 5.

It's partly his own fault, too busy mixing the album with Tony to go out and promote it, not even on *Top of the Pops*. And partly theirs, now held hostage by the Musicians' Union who insist every artist appearing must re-record their hit from scratch specially for the BBC. It's why David cancelled his performance on the show last autumn, upset they'd demanded he sing with the shonky strings of their own studio orchestra. This time in his absence it's left to Pan's People to make a short sexy dance of 'Rebel Rebel' in silver boots and bat capes, the one joy between an otherwise joyless jamboree of Alvin Stardust, Lena Zavaroni, Paper Lace and the Wombles – the kids' books that have become a kids' TV show, that have become cuddly toys, that have become chocolate bars, that have become a pop group featuring the son of Hattie Jacques and pals disguised as rat-faced yetis gurgling about litter picking. And they, too, outsell David.

'Are you selling something?'

'SELLING! Very good, very good! Eh? Eh? You're wicked, eh? Wicked, eh? Say no more!'

Sunday night, and on stage in Drury Lane Eric Idle elbows Terry Jones as the heaving Theatre Royal erupts. Up in the balcony sit the Chelsea boys, David and Mick, on the town with their old ladies, Angie and Bianca, to forget any competitive cares in an hour of parrot-thwacking lunacy with the Pythons.

But is Mick laughing at 'nudge! nudge!' or because David's 'Satisfaction' rip-off only reached 5 when his original made number 1?

And is David laughing at 'wink! wink!' or because he knows in a few days he'll be collecting his new album artwork from the man Mick still believes is working exclusively for the Stones?

Poor David, thinks Mick. *Silly sod.*

Poor Mick, thinks David. *Silly sod.*

And so they sit with their glittering wives, until the final curtain telling them and the rest of the audience to 'PISS OFF', each smug in his private thoughts as the catchphrases fly and the packed house bellows.

'SAY – NO – MORE!'

SIX

TROUBLE IN PARADISE. Six months after Big Biba opened on Kensington High Street its books are balancing like a surfer with rickets in a force ten gale. Hopes of a prosperous first winter have been decimated by the three-day week, blacked-out window displays, rail strikes severing all suburban footfall, restrictions on higher purchase and increased credit card repayments. Inside, every floor still sparkles like a luxury liner where drifting fur fondlers and coat strokers remain dreamily unaware any iceberg has been struck. But it has. Big Biba is sinking.

Up in the fifth-floor Rainbow Room, the bands play on. From California, the Pointer Sisters, whose thrift-store homage to the boogie-woogie bugling of the Andrews Sisters is so perfect a match for Biba's décor you'd swear they were drawn into the original floorplan. From closer to home, Cockney Rebel, whose mannered croaky am-dram now leads Jobriath and Leo Sayer in the critics' strawclutching league table of most likely 'new Bowie' for '74. And from Belgium, an unassuming balding man with a beard surveying the temporary exhibition of his paintings hanging around the walls, including a Last Supper scene with Elvis replacing Christ and one of the Rolling Stones dressed as Nazis, all tempting money over taste at £300 a pop.

A Thursday lunchtime finds an anxious Guy Peellaert in Biba preparing for this evening's champagne press launch for the UK publication of *Rock*

Dreams, his book of the surrounding fantasy images with text by Nik Cohn. Anxious not for fear no one will snap up his pictures but because of the brand-new painting, not on display, he's brought along with him. The *real* 'new Bowie' for '74 – the gatefold album sleeve commissioned by David who has just arrived in his red dungarees and hunter green hat to collect it.

The concept is all David's, assisted with custom photographs by his friend Terry O'Neill, manipulated by Guy through his own painstaking photo process involving collage and airbrush. Half-man, half-beast and Tod Browning's *Freaks*. A portrait of him lying naked on his stomach, human from the waist up but with the legs and genitals of a Great Dane. Behind him, squatting on their trotters, two deformed fat circus ladies and a sideshow sign for 'The Strangest Living Curiosities'.

Taking a deep breath, Guy nervously removes the mounted board from its protective cover. David neither blinks nor speaks. Guy swallows dryly. Then a sniff. Then a twitch of David's mouth. Then a shiny-eyed sparkle. *Wait till Mick sees THIS!*

'It's . . . fantastic!'

No other word for it. Guy has made the ultimate rock dream out of David's future nightmare, a graphic collar and nametag leashing *Diamond Dogs* with the shocking visual immediacy it deserves. The bark warning of the bite.

'I've got problems,' laughs David, pointing at his canine lower portions. 'I don't think I exactly look like that,' he adds. 'I suppose it could look like me if I was coming out of Hyde Park at three in the morning. But it doesn't matter. It's a great picture. But it seems as if I'm coming out of something. Actually . . .' He hesitates, tilting his head, sniffing sharply. 'I'm not sure whether I'm getting *out* of the darkness . . . or walking back into it . . .'

THE DARKNESS. Even as spring lawns light up with buttery yellow daffodils fluorescent as 100 watt bulbs, like an aggressive mould it finds its corner to fester. A nice fat one with no windows where it can suck on the nutrients of hundreds of human eyeballs, their moist fertile minds perfect breeding grounds for its malignant black spores.

In London, it finds five. Two in Leicester Square, two more nearby on Wardour Street and another on Shaftesbury Avenue. The censors have passed it, and even if *The Sun* predicts '*every nutter and child molester in town will queue up to see it*', even if the *Mirror* says it '*should be banned*', even if one of Mary Whitehouse's psalm-mumbling cronies from the Festival of Light has applied for a summons against Greater London Council for daring to show it, no one can stop it. Not the screaming, not the fainting, not the puking, not the early bolting to the exits, not the lines backing all the way to Chinatown. There are some, like Father Crehan, a Jesuit priest in Mayfair, who believe it to be God's best publicity since The Singing Nun. 'I would like everyone over 16 to see this film,' he says. 'Because I believe in diabolical interference, I think it important that the public should be made aware of the dangers in dabbling with the supernatural.' And there are others, like the Catholic newspaper *The Universe*, who can only pray '*it has an aroma which should keep decent patrons well clear of the box office*'. The aroma of hot popcorn dripping with sick.

The Exorcist is here.

One week after it opens, so is its star. Linda Blair is a 15-year-old schoolgirl from Connecticut. She was just 13 when she made the film and her character, Regan, an actress's daughter who becomes possessed by a demon, is meant to be 12. Linda is Osmonds-confident, fond of animals, especially horses, typically teen giggly and polite enough to withstand several days of belittling by the British press, all dying to know if she'll suddenly projectile vomit her ice cream or answer their next question with the breaking news their mother sucks cocks in hell. Much like the Catholic Church, they seem reluctant to accept *The Exorcist* as a mere celluloid fiction achieved with prosthetics, sound effects and cold pea soup. 'It's the same everywhere I go,' she shrugs, having been asked for the gazillionth time where her horns are. 'I just can't convince people I'm an ordinary kid.'

An ordinary kid. There's another just like her in Stockwell. The only difference between them being Linda earned $1,400 a week filming *The Exorcist* and Bernadette earns just three quid every Saturday helping out at a hair salon. Making tea, sweeping up, sorting out the pile of magazines. But it's enough. One day's work and she can already afford her date with destiny.

Mel Bush presents

DAVID CASSIDY

WHITE CITY STADIUM

SUNDAY, MAY 26th AT 8PM

BOX OFFICE OPENS SUN, 12 NOON. TKTS £2.20.

Two pounds and 20p. The small cost of a young girl's dream. And still enough change from her wages for a Wimpy and chips.

Lucky Bernadette – you *shall* go to the ball. No matter how much the grown-up papers keep fretting about 'weenybopper' hysteria. Like that rubbish in the *Standard* only the other day.

'*Such concerts should not be banned, but rather everyone connected with their organisation should be aware that the line dividing fun and disaster is very fine.*'

But what do *they* know, Bernadette? About music and romance. About the way your David makes you feel, lying every night on your embroidered floral bedspread, staring at the ceiling, his voice vibrating through the wooden headboard. About that bone-deep love you can't articulate but in the repeat playing of records and felt-tip love hearts and the hours you're willing to queue for a £2.20 concert ticket.

About whatever any teenage girl must do to try and find some light among all this oozing darkness . . .

THEY ARE MADE OF LIGHT. The way it sparkles off their dresses, their teeth, their nails, twisting on the ballroom stage of the May Fair Hotel, voices streaking the ceiling with Technicolor blues and reds like a choral aurora borealis. Watching from one of the corner tables, David is dazzled, just as he was when he first saw the Three Degrees in Amsterdam.

Their last bow is their new single, 'Year Of Decision', about making up your mind, setting yourself free and leaving the bad stuff alone if you get strung up on a Jones. A Jones strung up on being Bowie, David's mind is already made up. The paint is still wet on *Diamond Dogs*, and even as it dries Defries is busy booking up its accompanying coast-to-coast summer tour of the States like an army of one-armed bandits primed to spew their jackpots. David's year, 'The Year of the Diamond Dogs', has long been decided for him. Or had until he heard the Three Degrees sing sweet insurrection.

'*Come on, come on and join us, please!*'

He happily obliges. Up in their hotel room, among a champagne swill of similar admirers including company suits from CBS and a DJ from Coventry named Pete Waterman, David's cold bled-white fingers in turn grip the black warmth of Fay, Valerie and Sheila. They bat slow lashes at his compliments and softly answer his eager queries about the where, who and how the magic they make is cast: the songwriter-producers Kenny Gamble and Leon Huff, a house band known by the acronym 'MFSB' and a studio in Philadelphia named Sigma. 'Sigma,' repeats David, underlining it in his memory. And wide awake in his year of decision he knows he's going to make a soul record.

Ideally in Philly with the Three Degrees but, for now, he makes do with Barnes and the face of Freemans catalogue.

'*Can you heeeaaar me?*'

David's new song. A love song. A *soul* song. A song so emotionally exposing that rather than keep it for himself he offers it to his wee Glaswegian guinea pig. In the hit wake of 'The Man Who Sold The World', Lulu has been telling the papers she wants to make more records with David and has also been thinking an awful lot about God of late. Possibly she's confusing one with the other. But for all the brief good David's done reviving her pop career she is still, unwaveringly, the same old Lulu. Summer-season-in-Bournemouth-with-Roy-Hudd Lulu. Primetime-bank-holiday-BBC-special-with-Bruce-Forsyth Lulu. Shaking-her-bubble-perm-to-'Boom-Bang-A-Bang'-at-Blighty's-cabaret-in-Farnworth Lulu.

A blue Monday in Olympic, David does his best to shape her into his feeble hope of a Three-Degrees-in-one Lulu. But like itching powder on a silk sheet 'Can You Hear Me' is too smooth for a voice that scratchy. David listens to the playback sipping Thameswater coffee and hears every gaping mile between himself and Philadelphia. Three-and-a-half-thousand of them. The right song with the wrong singer in the wrong place. But it's not Olympic. It's not even London. It's England. It's all of Bowietannia.

And David is done with it.

GOODBYE TO ALL THIS. To infants chucking rubbish on Wimbledon Common vainly hoping they'll see the Wombles pick it up. To high street butchers offering free legs of lamb to the first housewife who streaks up to the counter. To the Wilkins of Reading, BBC lab rats in the first televised reality experiment, *The Family*. To a new Doctor Who and old repeats of *Star Trek*. To mad youths bludgeoning old ladies, swearing in the dock 'The Devil was in me'. To the vicar in Chalk Farm, still warning of 'bad vibrations' and the need to practise exorcism. To the first matinee of *The Exorcist* at 11 a.m. and the last showing of *Zardoz* finishing near midnight. To magazines with David's face on the cover and no interview inside. To '*How well do you know Bowie?*' quizzes and find-his-superfan competitions. To letters pages telling him he's '*the best thing since sliced bread*' one week and '*you make me sick to my stomach*' the next. To the country that would sooner buy 'Billy, Don't Be A Hero' than 'Rebel Rebel'. Goodbye to all this.

Leave Bowietannia stuck in its glam hamster wheel with old posters of Ziggy Stardust. Leave it dancing in Jilly's and graffitiing station walls. Leave it in the pierced ears of boys and the dyed quiffs upon girls. Leave it shoplifting from Boots and starving in the mirror. Leave it to the fans, copycats, fakes and imposters. Leave it to the gall of lookalike Henry, gurning next to '*IS THIS THE REAL DAVID BOWIE?*' on the cover of *Mirabelle*. Leave it to Cockney Rebel on *The Old Grey Whistle Test* and Queen on *Top of the Pops*, to *Here Come The Warm Jets* at 33⅓ and 'This Town Ain't Big Enough For Both Us' at 45. Leave it to wear itself out for months, years, however long it takes, until, stupefied by imitation, numbed by derivation, it wakes up and remembers David's first commandment. *Regeneration*. Leave it to kick over its own statues, storm its own winter palace, change lives with its own revolution in sound and style. Leave it to the kids of this Bowietannia to build themselves a better one.

Already, its faint tremors in the concrete not 800 yards from the last London address David will know as 'home'. The Chelsea boutique Too Fast To Live, Too Young To Die, once a haven of Teddy Boy drapes and biker leathers, but now Malcolm the owner and his partner Vivienne are making fashion from fetishism. Black miniskirts with chains and zips. Shiny patent heels spiked for sadomasochism. Vests spelling out 'ROCK' in chicken bones from the café over the road. Square T-shirts with handwritten script copied from an erotic novel by Alexander Trocchi, pre-torn across the chest or ripped to specification. And blinking at them in the middle of the otherwise empty shopfloor the slender hatted frame of David Bowie.

He squints at the words.

'*I groaned with pain as he eased the pressure . . .*'

One hand opening the flap of his shoulder bag, he turns and steps across to Malcolm by the till. Malcolm knows who he is and David foregoes the charade of pretending he doesn't, cutting to the chase by pulling out a photograph and placing it on the counter.

'Do you think you'd be able to make me a T-shirt?' says David. 'Out of this?'

Looking down, Malcolm sees a production still of James Dean from the movie *Giant*: Elizabeth Taylor crouching at his feet, a shotgun slung across his shoulders in a Christ-like pose.

Malcolm tilts his chin, screws up his nose, then shakes his head. 'We don't go in for that anymore,' he says, not impolitely. 'All that James Dean and Marilyn chic. That's getting old hat. Look.' He points over at the Trocchi T. 'What about that? Something a bit more . . . transsexual?'

David ums, nods, sniffs, and calmly places the picture back in his bag. He wanders back to the rails, slowly rifling through the hangers, gently rubbing the stitching. *God, he looks utterly alone*, thinks Malcolm. *Alone and completely miserable.*

Then, without another word, pulling his hat down, David hurries through the door and out onto the King's Road. Leaving ripped clothes, chicken bones and the future behind him.

HIS LAST NIGHT IN OAKLEY STREET. In the sunken pit in the centre of his white shagpile living room, David slumps on a silver cushion, greedily sucking a Gitane like a milkshake, blankly staring at the walls hung with other pictures of James Dean he hasn't tried turning into T-shirts yet.

Tomorrow he sets sail for America, via France: his passage, one way. Rumours that David will be ending his 'live retirement' to tour the States this summer were as good as confirmed in last week's *NME*. By the time it's made official he'll already be the other side of the North Atlantic. He's spent these last few days in London turning down TV offers, including Russell Harty, listening to the Three Degrees and packing his bags. Literally, with the help of Angie who'll be staying behind with Zowie, his new nanny, Marion, their friends and her lovers. Mentally, with sharpening powder and an even sharper pair of scissors. The final severing of all bonds to Bowietannia. The ones that have been tickling his neck for much too long. But with a courageous sniff and a decisive snip the straggly dyed red locks tumble to the floor.

Ta-ta, Ziggy.

He runs his hand over his nape, the back of his hair now curving to a stop in an even shelf at the collar. A hard look in the mirror. The thin white face with its crimson hair brushed flat in a side parting. He smiles to himself.

'Is that really *YOU*?'

AND THEN HE'S GONE. Without send-off, without ceremony, without anyone noticing he's no longer here. Just business as usual in the obliviously Bowieless new Bowietannia.

Another week with the Carpenters' album at number 1 and another Grand National win for Red Rum. Another Saturday evening watching *The Black and White Minstrel Show* and another Sunday reading about sex changes in the papers. Another jump in the price of petrol and another coupon to save 2p on a box of oxtail soup powder. Another magazine with a letter from '*a disillusioned Bowie freak*' and another Miners make-up ad showing a girl in her bedroom with David's face on her wall.

Another property viewing in Kensington and another phone call to a suite in the Savoy Hotel. Another script in the hands of Richard Harris and another lost place on the page as he picks up the receiver. Another grin as he's told it's five times what he paid for it and another 'good man' as he hangs up. Another month before he's finished filming *Juggernaut* but only five days before he's back in the society pages of the *Daily Mail*.

'*A canny man is Richard Harris, behind the bombast and carefully cultivated image of a hellraiser. He has resituated himself, taking a profit on his Kensington home. The price was more than £350,000 for the ghost-ridden folly which Harris, 40, bought seven years ago for about £75,000.*

Rock star David Bowie (of the dual persona) was just beaten in the race to buy the six-bedroom Gothic tower house by the equally exotic Jimmy Page, guitarist with the Led Zeppelin group.

"David Bowie came to look a couple of times," says Harris. "But he was a little slow in making up his mind" . . .'

SEVEN

IT'S A GOOD PLACE TO GO MAD. It has previous form, and very recent. Four months ago this was the curtained asylum of Howard Hughes – the ninth floor of the Inn on the Park where he spent his year in London rotting on a diet of Valium, codeine and milk-based desserts, watching films in the nude, in the dark, day and night. Today, the drapes are open, its inner luxury seen anew in the light of a misty grey Thursday morning. But its bathroom tiles still echo with lunacy.

'That's it . . . I've had it.'

From the lips of a dark curly-haired pop star, gazing at his bugged-out reflection in the mirror above the sink. He's talking to his manager, sat on the edge of the bath behind him, calmly rolling him a joint, who tells him: 'Don't be silly.'

The star trembles.

'After tonight, I'm out.' His tone is soft but defiant. 'I'm pissed off with being locked up in hotel rooms waiting for room service.'

The manager laughs dismissively.

The star snaps. 'You're like the wardens!'

Then sits down on the toilet seat opposite him.

'It's all right for *them*. At least they don't have to play at being the clown. See, I'm on stage for a whole hour tonight and I have to play at being Judy Garland. I jump when they say jump. I spend enough time in fucking planes and bathrooms, hiding from people that I made rich!'

The manager hands him the joint. 'Here,' he says. 'Try that.'

A second's silence.

'AND CUT!'

The manager looks over to the cluster of bodies standing behind the camera. 'That all right, cock? Or do you need us to do it again?'

'No, that's great,' says the director. 'Thanks, Adam. Thanks, David.'

Adam Faith, who'd still much prefer everyone call him 'Terry', stands up, stretching his arms.

The prop joint still in his hand, his curly-wigged co-star waves it at the crew with a toothy smile and a twinkle in his eye the size of the Hope Diamond.

'Anyone want this?'

David Essex cracks jokes on set every chance he gets. He needs to. Only a few more weeks of filming left, and art and life are becoming scarily symbiotic.

On the back of last year's *That'll Be the Day*, he became a Top 10 pop star. Number 3 with 'Rock On', voted one of *Petticoat*'s 'Most Beautiful Men', the Christmas cover of *Jackie* dressed as Santa and endless magazine fact files.

'*Dark brown hair, dark blue eyes, stands 5 foot 10½ inches, weighs 10 stone, likes quiet people, honey, fairy stories, Indian food, chocolate, flowers (especially red roses), the countryside, tap-dancing and the Marx Brothers, dislikes smoking, sports cars, arrogance, laziness, bad manners, too much make-up on girls and grand opera.*'

This year's sequel, *Stardust*, is about how becoming such a pop star will send any normal human being completely doolally. It's written by music journalist Ray Connolly, a seasoned expert in rock'n'roll headbangers long before he interviewed David Bowie last year for the *Evening Standard*. Whereas David Essex is a happy 26-year-old husband and father and not remotely mad. At least he didn't think he was. Not until he started shooting *Stardust*.

The producers have been exploiting his fame as a real life *Popswop* pin-up to film scenes of fans going berserk for his character, Jim MacLaine. The shoot started in February outside a crematorium in Northolt where

Jim gets mobbed and the genuine stampede of Essex-eyed teens made it only too convincing. When the location moved to Manchester, members of his fan club were recruited to fill the Belle Vue Kings Hall, the director begging them to chant 'We want Jim!' as they bawled and fainted for 'DAVID!' Every other day on set there's usually a reporter from one of the teen mags, there to grab words with David Essex in the off-camera hours between his next scene as a harassed Jim MacLaine sick of media intrusion. He smiles and does his best to give them the Cockney gypsy dreamboat they want, the one whose syrupy eyes could make Mother Theresa lie spread-eagled naked shaking her feet in the air. But these past few weeks his twinkle is rapidly dulling. Every scene in the can, David feels a little less David, a little more Jim. A little more ever so slightly loose at the screws.

He steps over wires, light stands and cameramen's feet, out into the lounge where Adam is leafing through today's *FT*, over to the balcony patio doors with their view over Park Lane traffic. Black cabs, lorries, red double-decker buses. The normal world.

It's only a movie, he tells himself. *I am an actor, I'm not Jim. He's just my character. My name is David. I'm married to Maureen. I'm the father of Verity. It's only a movie. It's only a movie!*

Only a movie. Except when it wraps after the final 'CUT!', David Essex will still be a pop star.

EIGHT

NEW YORK CITY. David's been coming here for three years, passing in and out like a threading needle. But this is where he knots the stitch. This time it's home.

A knot on the southeast corner of Central Park, the Sherry-Netherland hotel where he wakes staring at the recessed ceiling of an elegantly furnished three-bedroom apartment, his skinny white limbs entwined like a candy cane with the skinny black ones of his lover.

Ava's been waiting for him here ever since Angie extradited her overseas, for the last month racking up a separate Midtown hotel bill at the expense of Mainman: officially as a signed artiste in development; unofficially as his mistress on the payroll. Now that he's here she'll cling to him everywhere he goes like a zip coat, absent only in the occasional states of emergency when Mrs Bowie flies into town and the rules of whatever deadly game their marriage has become require Ava to hide in the nearest cloakroom until the all-clear.

The one hankering Ava can't satisfy, the door of an eccentrically decorated apartment off Madison Avenue can. Home to a social charmer named Norman dealing in art and 'snow' with the same eye for quality, often trading like for like. David has nothing to barter but disposable wealth and his association. Norman is happy to collect both in exchange for as many kilos as David needs to keep blinkless pace with the breakneck metropolis.

In the city he already knows he is only too easily found. The bar-tab city of conspicuous queens and respectable junkies, the preen-to-be-seen city of Max's and Kenny's Castaways and balcony seats in Carnegie Hall, the gossipy cocktail city of aftershows with the overtalented stick insect Todd Rundgren and the unfoldingly tragic Dolls, and their private booths sardined between bony fidgeting men and beautiful glassy-eyed women icily pretending David's change of haircut isn't the biggest newsflash since Patty Hearst got kidnapped. But he can only blow smoke so long at the same old faces, old flames and old foes singing the same old songs, wanting him to be the same old David.

Itching for a different tempo, he needs new cubicles to visit.

They're waiting for him Uptown. In El Barrio, where the Latin roses shake sensually to live merengue rhythms on the floor of the Corso club, and further up in Harlem where the wing collars of the Detroit Spinners flap in unison like a flock of gulls as they skip onto the stage of the world-famous Apollo. Limousined back and forth to the thresholds of both, a cool white prince observing effortlessly cooler paupers, David falls in love with all of it. The congas, the brass, the moves, the legs, the suits, the shoes, the brownness, the blackness, the music, the music, the music, the music. Music which has the same effect on his brain as Norman's powder, shooting rockets down his spine, igniting his hips like a napalm airstrike. And he isn't alone.

Beneath twinkling mirror balls way beyond Manhattan, the hips of America blaze with similar motion. Not two months ago its number 1 single was Barry White's cloud nine mating dance 'Love's Theme' by his Love Unlimited Orchestra. The April David arrives, the Sigma studio house band MFSB follow it there with 'TSOP' – 'The Sound Of Philadelphia' – adapted from their theme to the black music show *Soul Train* and featuring the haloed tones of the Three Degrees. So a revolution begins, right under the nose of white Watergate America with its crooked presidents, kidnapped heiresses, freckly Waltons and curlered Carpenters. A declaration of independence written in four-on-the-floor and the chatterbox *tchs* of a puckering hi-hat, setting out the sacred tribal rites of the new Saturday night. A revolution for now with no name until somebody realises 'disco' doesn't only have to mean the building where strangers gather to dance but the sound of the dance itself. The one truly indigenous music of Seventies America. And it's black as the hair dye in Nixon's bathroom cabinet.

And the body glistening between David's sheets as he rolls off her, damp with the moisture of their frantic union. The same black skin he'll see when his eyelids unstick tomorrow after sleep has wrung out the last echoes of dancing till dawn, coming to with a dull ache between his ears worse than the one between his legs and a sinking in his gut like a bellboy's knocked on his forehead bearing a bad telegram.

DAVID STOP LIFE ISN'T ALL SEX SOUL AND MAMBOS STOP REMEMBER THE REASON WHY YOU'RE IN NEW YORK CITY IN THE FIRST PLACE STOP

He remembers. Oh, god, he remembers. He has a job to do. Stop.

SIXTY MILES FROM NEW YORK CITY LIES ANOTHER. A city within a city in a warehouse on the Jersey banks of the Delaware River, still under construction by men cursing with drills and brushes and toolbelts and steel toecaps, made out of aluminium and wood and cloth and paper and paint and plastic wiring. A flatpack city to be erected and dismantled on a daily basis by a 30-strong crew, big enough that it will take three enormous trailer trucks to transport in a convoy the length of several cricket pitches. Once finished it will stand a spiky 40 feet high, a wonky 100 feet wide and a concertinaed 60 feet deep. A schoolkid might eye up its grey skyscrapers with big splotches of red and yellow and say it looks like something from a Spiderman comic. An art critic might skew their neck following its hard jagged angles and say it looks like something by the Vorticists. They'd both be right. It's an abstract cartoon of a city, one not to be lived in but looked at, with a catwalk bridge that moves up and down and an extendable hydraulic arm designed with the sole purpose of dangling David Bowie above the screaming heads of his audience: a carrot-haired man on an actual stick. Because this is his city, 'Hunger City' from *Diamond Dogs*. And once they're finished building it he's going to have to live in it.

The architecture isn't David's, only the concept, as loosely briefed to an ill-looking Broadway lighting designer named Jules and his set maker, Mark. A brief born out of conversations about the staging of his next tour that began many weeks ago in London before the clocks sprung forward, when daylight, hope and electricity were still in short supply and David tempered his pessimism about humanity's future in chalkdusted thoughts of nuclear war, *Metropolis* and Adolf Hitler. A David who had yet to castrate Ziggy's hair, meet the Three Degrees or learn to stop worrying and love the bomb. A different David to the one now no longer quite so sure if he still wants the key to Hunger City.

It used to be The Dream. Rock'n'roll as theatre. Proper theatre, with lights and scenery, every movement carefully blocked and choreographed, every song not played as a singer but *performed* as an actor. David had his moments on stage with the Spiders, but nothing to match the scale of the footlit ambitions he hoped to satisfy with the wayside Orwell and Ziggy musicals. Ambitions now transferred like the swapping of engines to his 'Year of the Diamond Dogs' tour.

And so the sketchbook meetings with Jules and Mark, and the hammering of nails in a warehouse in Lambertville. And the procession of candidates marching in and slouching out of a fifth-floor studio off Sixth Avenue.

You can't stage a musical without musicians, and David needs to fill up his equivalent orchestra pit. Those who audition do so under the delusion that if they succeed they will have joined 'David Bowie's new band'. But there is no such thing. There is a show called 'The Year of the Diamond Dogs' and there is its star, David Bowie, and that is all. The names of anyone he thinks good enough to tinkle the keys, tap the cymbals, pluck the strings and toot the horns is immaterial. Because they are not members of a group. They are drones on an assembly line. They will learn to play every song like they were barrel pianos, never deviating or improvising, and they will stand where X marks their spot so far back on the stage it may as well be the loading bay. If they're lucky, they might get their name in small type in a tour programme and enough kudos to warm the sheets of a Holiday Inn with glitter-blind girls so in love with the organ grinder they're willing to fuck any one of his umpteen monkeys. But even if some of them are old faithfuls, like his pianist Garson, or his longtime session bassist Herbie, none of them will suffer any spotlight burn. The greatest lesson the Spiders ever taught David is that he's done with the stress of being 'a band'. The naïve belief that camaraderie somehow means equality. The bitter showdowns about

57

pennies and percentages. The jealousies, the mutinies, the backstabbings, the dangers of another Mick Ronson treading on his toes and leeching off his limelight. Never again.

David only wants a ring where he can be master and caged animals who'll skip to his whip. He wants The Year of the Diamond Dogs to be a one-man show. And he wants a vodka tonic.

Next door to his rehearsal studio, at the Savoy on West 44th where the bar-propping dockers don't know him from Adam, or Eve now they take a closer look. But 'the drinks are on me' and their slaps break his shoulder blades.

'Yeah, you're OK, mac, you're one a da guys!'

And so they leave David and whoever his companion is that day alone, sipping regularly, sniffing occasionally, smoking constantly. Thinking always. Asking himself –

Whether it's still worth all this bother trying to reinvent the rock concert?

Whether, this time, he'll finally conquer America?

Whether he'll ever have a hit record over here, even if sung by someone else?

Whether he should still try and get a song to Elvis Presley, or focus on a younger teen idol, maybe that David Cassidy?

Whether he should bother finishing that soul record he started in London with Lulu?

Whether to scrap the lot and make a new soul record of his own?

Whether Ava's crazy enough to think she's in love with him?

Whether he and Angie will last?

Whether he needs to ring Norman?

Whether he has enough of *it* on him?

Or whether to order another drink?

Yes . . . another vodka tonic.

Sniff.

Right after a quick visit to the bathroom . . .

NOT ONE MILE from the ice cubes rattling at the bottom of David's glass, as a thick brittle stub of grey ash drops with a noiseless tap into his ashtray,

Tony Defries shifts back in his office chair and contemplates the size of David's cock and balls.

'The offending articles.'

That's what his record company are calling them. Not his actual cock and balls – by unanimous eyewitness testimony 'the splendid articles' – but the ones hanging between the hindquarters of the painted dog's body on David's new album cover. By any measure, masculine or canine, they are not an especially big cock and balls. You can't even see them properly. Just a dangling blob that could be a flaccid dog's dick or a flash of its scrotum but nothing anyone would ever consider approaching the realms of bestial pornography. Anyone apart from RCA. In their latest memo that's just wafted on to Defries's desk, they now insist that, for decency's sake, doggie David be castrated by airbrush.

He takes a languid, contemplative puff. *The offending articles?*

There are more spread out on his desk. Today's poker hand of invoices, letters, telexes and magazines. Many of them bills and costings for the upcoming tour. The one that looks like it might cost as much as a quarter of a million dollars, but since all expenses are deducted from David's share of earnings Defries isn't especially worried. He hasn't really seen much of David since he docked in New York, leaving him be to do whatever he has to do, at work and play, so long as he's ready for the opening night in Montreal in a few weeks' time. Defries's only input is to make sure any musicians he hires are paid the bare minimum and to push up the ticket prices to the absolute maximum. Basic Mainman economics. It's never about the product. The art is in the sell.

Like the great big sell Defries has just got going on the corner of Seventh and 47th. Bigger than the Jobriath billboard that used to hang opposite, which is what gave him the idea in the first place. All those Times Square pimps and pushers craning up at a seven-storey-high ad for a new album by someone they've never heard of called Mick Ronson. Only the queer thing about it is the main portrait painting looks nothing like Ronson but *exactly* like someone else. A young man with a bare chest, shaggy brown hair and a beaming smile. And there's not a gum-smacking chicken on the deuce who doesn't see it.

'Mick *who*? Aw, now ain't dat s'posed to be David Cassidy?'

★

THERE'S NO POINT PAINTING HIM. Fans try but they can never capture those eyes, that smile, those dimples with brushes, pencils or felt-tips the way a camera can like the cover of last week's *Jackie*.

'HAPPY BIRTHDAY, DAVID!'

And this year his birthday would have to fall on Good Friday. The holy day of J.C. and all Bernadette could think about was D.C.

And the Lord burdened us with the sins of all of us!

Jesus died at three o'clock, and by four, there she was, eating a Super Mousse with her pals, giggling over his horoscope.

'*David's Scorpio-Aries personality makes him enjoy being admired by lots of girls and I'm sure he really enjoys the idea that so many of us are head over heels in love with him!*'

Head over heels over head and heels again. In her thin box bedroom Bernadette grips her pencil tightly. Not a portrait, but an essay for a school project on pristine ruled paper. She writes neatly and knowledgably. For 14, she writes well.

> To be exact David Bruce Cassidy – his full name – was born on the dot at 10 a.m. on the 12th April 1950. The place was the Flower Fifth Hospital in New York City. His parents were actress Evelyn Ward and the singer/actor Jack Cassidy. Because his father was in show business, more often than not he was away from home. Evelyn was left all alone with little David and she often felt sad, lost and very lonely. This got unbearable and Jack and Evelyn split up and finally – divorce. What an ugly word! Poor David!

Ugly divorce. A good Catholic is Bernadette, even if she does worship graven images. Only five weeks now to White City. They've all got tickets, Bernadette and her best friends Margaret and Vanda. 'You're David Cassidy mad!' says her mum, but it's her money and she's only young once and if the Lord Jesus doesn't tell her enough, there's always the new number 1 vibrating her radio. Have joy, have fun. A Jacques Brel ballad sung by a Canadian named Terry with a voice like a sock puppet.

'*Goodbye, my friend, it's hard to die!*'

Bernadette, very much alive, full of joy, full of fun, full of everything a teenage girl should be, opens her bedside drawer to look at the ticket for the thousandth time. She holds it delicately between finger and thumb, ever so gently rubbing it, just to make sure it's real. 'SUNDAY, 26th MAY'. Five weeks away. Five weeks and she'll be there, and *he'll* be there. In the same place on Earth, at the same time, breathing the same West London oxygen. And with the ticket still in her hand, in her small Stockwell bedroom she wonders, as she always wonders, sat on top of her covers, under his face, pinned by that smile.

I wonder what my David is doing right now?

NINE

HE'S DASHING FROM the back of a limousine, feet barely touching the sidewalk before he's safely past the doorman. No crowds to dodge as nobody knows he's here, just Fifth Avenue pedestrians all much too busy watching the traffic, the lights or their feet to take much notice of a small, slim figure masked by large sunglasses darting under a hotel entrance canopy. But with a face this famous, habit is habit.

The shades stay on even inside the foyer. A long, thin hall with chandeliers hanging from an ornately decorated barrel-vaulted ceiling, highback wingchairs, brass standard lamps and an alcove reception desk. Tight beside him, just bolted from the same car, stands his security man. He sees her first. The young woman who's been waiting for them, slowly approaching with narrow eyes, a broad nose and an efficient smile. She outstretches a hand. 'David,' she says without nerves, like it's an answer, not a question. He shakes it with a 'Hi' and a smile warmer than hers merits but, again, habit is habit. Then, with 'I'll take you on up' and the echo of practical heels clicking on the tiled mosaic floor she leads them businesslike to the nearest elevator.

It's only then, once the doors slide shut, that he removes and folds away his sunglasses. It gives him something to do while the floor lights blink and his bodyguard small-talks on his behalf, the efficient young woman still nodding with the same fixed smile, expending as little energy as she

62

can. Until with a soft *ping!* the elevator stops and out they step, her heels muted by green carpet, heading left towards a white door which she knocks once as a formality before turning the handle. Not having been told otherwise, they follow her inside.

The smell of exotic flowers, or maybe perfume, and lingering smoke. Through another door into soft light, expensive-looking furniture, a baby grand piano, a mess of records tossed like playing cards on the carpet by a stereo and a black woman with shaved dyed peroxide hair with one eye on the magazine in her lap and another on one of two television sets. Passing on to another door, ajar, which the efficient woman knocks twice. 'Wait here,' she whispers, slipping in for all of five seconds before reappearing.

'He'll see you now,' she says and, pushing the door open, they see him then.

Dressed a bit like a Harlem pimp, loose cotton trousers and an open white shirt with wing collars tickling the edge of his bony shoulders. His hair is swept to the right in a ruffled orangey mop, a silver bangle on his left wrist, a smouldering cigarette tweezered in his right fingers. He saunters over to greet them, face thin as a closed pair of bellows, a skew-whiff smile, his eyes glassy.

'David,' says David Bowie.

'David,' says David Cassidy.

And the world spins ever more strangely.

The two Davids sink into two davenports pushed together into an L as the bodyguard settles in a chair in the corner. The efficient woman floats in between them offering drinks. 'A beer' for David Bowie. 'Make that two' for David Cassidy. A rain check for the bodyguard. Refreshments supplied, she exits noiselessly, pulling the door not quite shut.

David Bowie offers David Cassidy a cigarette. He smiles, thinks, hesitates, declines.

David Bowie sniffs, runs his tongue over his gums and lights another.

David Cassidy sips his drink. Everyone in the room hears the gulp.

'So . . .' David Bowie begins.

So, indeed.

So they sit, eye to eye, pin-up to pin-up, man of 27 to man of just-turned-24. Knowing nothing about one another besides the little they've read or been told and the music they've heard on the radio or seen performed on TV.

Music.

Music has done this. Music has brought David Cassidy on a plane all the way from his Encino ranch home outside Los Angeles to a suite in the Sherry-Netherland in New York City for a conference with David Bowie.

Music has planted the idea somewhere in David Bowie's fertile head between sex, drugs, Barry White and Adolf Hitler that he needs a new artist to produce, another Lulu to play with, and that Lulu could be American teen idol David Cassidy.

Music, with its 'what if?' zillion-to-one possibilities and none more boggling than the zillion-to-one possibility that the voice of David Cassidy singing the music of David Bowie could be something precious, mysterious and amazing. Because why wouldn't it? The voice of 'How Can I Be Sure' blacksmith hammered to the contours of a 'Life On Mars?' or 'Rock 'N' Roll With Me'. The Trojan horse of a 'Time' or 'We Are The Dead' rolling into the bedrooms of millions upon millions of teenage girls on the wheels that sang 'Daydreamer'. The chance for one to change his image once and for all by making the sort of music he hasn't been allowed to make in nearly four years of being cuddly kissable Keith Partridge. The chance for the other to have a smash hit in America for the first time in nearly three years of being freaky faggy Ziggy Stardust.

'So . . .'

So they sit, in a moment so fragile it could change pop music for the rest of the decade, maybe the rest of time depending on what either says, or doesn't say, in however long it takes before one of them decides the conversation which hasn't properly started yet is well and truly over. A conversation between two fame-fucked superstars acutely aware they've already spent too much of their lives in planes and bathrooms hiding from people they've made rich.

David Bowie, who last year quit touring, who this year for reasons of art and ego and money is returning to the screams and the lights and the madness.

David Cassidy, who has had enough of the screams and the lights and the madness, who no longer needs the money, who this year for reasons of trying to avoid a straitjacket has decided that his next month of dates in Europe will be his last.

David Bowie, who could tell David Cassidy everything about planning, or even faking, a retirement, how not to tell the press beforehand but pull the pin from the grenade during the very last encore then stand back and watch a fanbase explode.

David Cassidy, who could tell David Bowie everything about the perils of going back in again, because fame, as he knows after 96 episodes, 11 albums and a Rice Krispies commercial, is not a game anyone can play on their own terms but a petted dog that licks your hand until the day it bites your arm off.

'So . . .'

So they sit, pretending to appreciate what's at stake, what one can do for the other, what worlds they could conquer and epochs they could start, yet both of them failing, neither pushing nor pulling, each too consciously trapped playing the same version of themselves because they've forgotten how to play anyone else.

David Bowie, hiding behind his lukewarm, sniffy, chainsmokey, 'cor blimey', not afraid of silences, cagily testing the intellectual mettle David Bowieness.

David Cassidy, stuck in his cutely grinning, puka shell-necklaced, lightly stoned, son of a *Columbo* villain, trying very hard so the world doesn't see how stark raving insane he is David Cassidyness.

Just two strangers becoming ever more so with each slow mistrusting second.

'So . . .'

So?

So let history record that one day in late April 1974 in New York City David Bowie meets David Cassidy. They sit and they talk, and, after a while, David Bowie plays David Cassidy a couple of songs he'd like him to sing: one by Lou Reed, the other his own 'Growing Up And I'm Fine' as already recorded by Mick Ronson. David Cassidy listens, asks a few questions, passes politely noncommittal compliments and finishes his drink with a tongue parched for twenty more. Then he stands up, his bodyguard mirroring his every move, says 'It's been a pleasure' and 'Goodbye' and 'I'll give you a call'. And before he's out the door David Bowie knows he'll never see him again.

The efficient woman takes them back to the lobby, having rung ahead to make sure David Cassidy's driver is there waiting out front.

The sunglasses are on before he's in the elevator and stay on until the car door slams. A minute later it swings round onto 59th, gliding by the Plaza before turning onto Seventh, down, down all the way through Times Square, past the trash-raking hags and the tatty-furred whores squinting at the new billboard on the corner of 47th. The one for the new album by David Bowie's old guitarist. And if only he wasn't distracted by doubt and confusion and the huge *Great Gatsby* hoarding across the street, David Cassidy might even agree it looks exactly like him.

THE EFFICIENT WOMAN. She knows she is. She's proud of it. Efficiency has got her where she is, which is precisely where she wants to be.

With him, every day.

It just so happened that when the situation came up there didn't seem to be any other candidate. It could never be Angie because Angie is The Wife. It can't be Suzi anymore as she's gone off with Mick Ronson. It could be wild gal Cherry Vanilla, still here on the Mainman payroll and writing weekly 'My World' columns for *Mirabelle* on David's behalf. But lately strange events have conspired to cast Cherry in an unreliable light. Like she can't do her job anymore, like she needs to be replaced. And so a vacuum appears and, right on cue, in she steps with her brown clothes and practical shoes and bulletproof dedication. The efficient woman to save the day. He even asks her personally.

'Corinne, would you . . . ?'

She would. Drop her life in London like a bag of groceries, come to New York and work for him. Be at his beck and call every minute of every day from this day forward, for better, for worse, for richer, for poorer, in sickness and in health, till death do us part.

'I do!'

Therefore, I now pronounce you boss and employee. You may kiss the personal assistant.

Mwah!

The new routines she learns fast. She is the butler with his morning coffee and orange juice and the latest papers and music magazines. She is the secretary with the day's appointments, reserver of tables, requester of tickets, caller of room service, arranger of cars, tracker of deliveries, planner of all side entrances and back exits. She is the ratcatcher who can smell vermin journalists at twenty paces and hers the pleasure of keeping all notepads, recorders and cameras out of his face. She is the second 'no' to every interview request if Defries hasn't said it first. She is the shrewd ingratiator, tiptoeing around the inner hierarchy of friends and lovers, the Freddies and Avas, his bodyguard Stuey, his driver Jim 'The Lim', Angie's voice on the end of a telephone or whichever fagged-out body is snoring beside him. She is the stanchion gripping the velvet rope between him and the outside world, admitting only the privileged few with the secret password. And it is now up to her who knows it. Everything else is instinct, animal cunning and red-alert self-preservation. What she isn't supposed to see, she doesn't and, trusting her not to, David hides nothing. One mistake – one late limo, one forgotten phone call, one wrong interloper, one indiscretion, one leak, one syllable of gossip in the press with her saliva on it – and she could be on the next plane home. But she is Corinne. She doesn't make any.

Tonight is textbook. She makes sure Jim has the car there on time to take him and his small party, including herself, the short ride down to West 43rd where his old friends Fanny are playing the Town Hall. Not quite the same Fanny he first met last summer, the image glitterier, the music rockier and with half the original line-up gone replaced by two new members including Suzi Quatro's big sister Patti on guitar. But David's sometime Filipino lover, Jean, is still up front on bass, legs and lips, singing her new song inspired by recent nights of bed-breaking sex with someone '*hard as a rock*' who can make it all night long. It's called 'Butter Boy'. David doesn't even blush.

When the concert finishes, the car is there, just as Corinne synchronised, to return to the Sherry with however many extra passengers he chooses. Then, up in his suite, as the music plays and the drinks pour and the pupils dilate, she keeps her sharpest eye on who's present, just in case they shouldn't be, and a blinder one to the movements of his little silvery spoon. Until the only part of the job she doesn't particularly care for. When David disappears, never alone, and a bedroom door closes behind him. And she is left on the other side of it. But she can live with it.

Because tomorrow Jean will be gone, just like all the others go, yet she'll still be here. Precisely where she wants to be.

With him. *Every* day.

DON'T DO IT, DEREK. Please, don't. It's a bad idea. A very, very bad idea. You're a respectable man of 31. You're a primary teenager, you have a wife, you have three daughters and you could lose it all if you go ahead with this. Because it won't work. All that's going to happen is people will think you've gone nuts. The school for sure, and if not them, then the parents of the kids you teach. You will be mocked in the street. Ridiculed by the papers. Struck off by the education committee. So, please, Derek. Please! *Don't do it.*

He does it.

Of course he does it. Because even under the bluest skies, as the wireless gaily shakes with Wombling remembrance and ABBA's 'Waterloo', even as the estates ring with children's cheers and the shrill metal peel of 'Popeye The Sailor Man' heralding the ice-cream van, even in the first sugary Orange Maid suck of summer the darkness still demands its season in the sun.

It's *The Exorcist*. It makes people do all sorts of strange things. *Bad* things. In Portsmouth a naval cadet who sees the film is found dead two nights later, having thrown himself out of a barracks window in his sleep. On the Isle of Wight it's blamed for the suicide of a 15-year-old-girl. In York its name crops up among the possible culprits in an inquest into the accidental overdose of a Black Sabbath fan. In Hull cinema queuers are handed out leaflets with emergency help numbers for seven local priests. On its opening night in Bridgend a local Pentecostal minister is called in to help ambulancemen sedate a housewife driven to hysterics.

And then there's Derek.

He teaches a class of 7-year-olds in Letchworth but in his spare time he likes to paint. His latest work is called 'The Exorcism of a Superstar'. Derek thinks it's a good painting. No, Derek thinks it's a *great* painting. So great he thinks it deserves to be hung in a local church, only, so far, three separate vicars have refused him. 'They say they don't think a church is the place for it to hang,' he broods. 'I disagree.'

Which is when he gets his very bad idea. That he could win over the public and force the clergy to reconsider if he staged a clever publicity stunt.

So he does. On a busy Saturday afternoon, in the centre of Luton, on George Street just outside the ABC where they're screening *The Exorcist*. Where Derek, dressed in priest's robes and with the help of his whole family, performs his own public exorcism against the backdrop of his painting, pride of place, propped against the cinema entrance.

As his wife circulates among the crowd trying to gather signatures on a petition, Derek waves a burning crucifix over the heads of their three daughters, stood on the pavement, each in their own separate chalk circle holding a piece of bread dripping with wine. Placed around them, at their feet, are church candles, some human bones and a cereal bowl near full to the brim. With their father's piss.

Derek never does get his painting accepted by the church. Only a month's suspension from his teaching post. And one day's tabloid infamy as the '*macabre*' artist responsible for, as described: '*A picture showing Christ on a cross with a bishop giving a V-sign to him, surrounded by various pop stars past and present, including a portrait of David Bowie, with female breasts.*'

THERE IS ANOTHER KING IN EXILE. Also recently absconded from Bowietannia. Not that he'd have called it that. Because if it was ever anyone's country, he knows, it was his. Once. Not so very long ago, when one sparkle of his sequins on even the smallest television screen was all it took to turn sad froglike children in the ugliest houses in the rainiest towns in the dreariest shires of mothballed Englandshire into the prince or princess of their own terraced fairy tales. When his was the revolution and the thump in the heart of every kid singing its song. When Britain belonged to Marc.

Bolantannia! The promised land of glam. The Seventies' teen salvation he created without knowing what he was doing, without knowing what to call it. And for a long time nor did anybody else. And then, one summer at the very pinnacle of his reign, they did. And then it could be weighed, bought and sold. And thus manhandled the shine was ruined. And like a rainbow-furred cat leaping out of its bag only to be skinned alive by the steak knives of commerce, it died in agony. And now all that's left in the charts is the buzzing of flies over dried blood. And the spunk of teenage boys wanking over Suzi Quatro in her black leather catsuit. And nobody wanking over Alvin Stardust in his black leather catsuit. And everyone wanking over ABBA's Agnetha in her blue satin knickerbocker suit. And Sparks turning up too late like a camp cavalry to save a battle already lost. And Mud wondering how come the toddlers who buy their jelly-and-blancmange music haven't noticed they must have the combined age of 209. And The Sweet trying too hard to *be* hard by dressing like Steppenwolf and acting like all that Wig-Wam-Coco-crap was part of a cunningly duplicitous long game just so one day they'd get to play heavy metal on *Crackerjack*. And Slade reduced to being Sad Slade, the tears-behind-the-laughter Slade, the stomplessly wistful where-have-all-the-good-times-gone Slade of depressing singles like 'Everyday'. And David Bowie, nowhere to be seen except in echoes of his old haircut bopping along every high street. And sporting a pair of tits in a painting by a nutcase.

And Marc. Not giving up, just moving on. Moving away from the country that's forsaken him, where his latest album spluttered to number 12 and his latest single wheezed to 13, where he's been on fewer magazine covers this year than David Essex, where the collapse of his marriage is the worst-kept secret in the pop gossip columns, where the new Finance Act currently passing through parliament is about to reduce his annual tax bill to a plea for bankruptcy. The country he last played across six dates this January in a tour he named 'Truck Off', as in 'fuck off!' – to the critics who say he's become '*a coked-up Bob Dullard*', to the stale cries of 'sell-out!' still stinking up letters pages, to the shrinking size of his interview features, to the taxman, to divorce lawyers, to any chart position other than 1, to the puppets of ChinniChapp, to Björn and Benny and Uncle Bulgaria and the whole bastard lot of them. And so, just like David, he goes.

Just like David, to America. Just like David, with a black American lover. Just like David, unable to last a day without ramrodding a biscuit tin's worth of tropane alkaloids up his sinuses. Just like David, evangelical about making his next album a funky black soul album, which is why he's about to head back to his favourite studio off Hollywood Boulevard, only a cowboy's campfire fart from where *Blazing Saddles* spins six times a day at Grauman's Chinese Theatre.

But first, New York.

A city Marc loves, unrequited, but that goes for the rest of America. He's never been able to fathom it. How come it still loves Alf Garnett, as Archie Bunker, and Albert Steptoe, as Fred G. Sanford, but it only loved him for all of two weeks in '72 when 'Get It On' was a Top 10 hit. Then dumped him for Gilbert O'Sullivan, leaving him to the ballpark heckles playing tour support to Three Dog Night. Because for every Elton John who makes it here, there are another twenty Slades who don't. Yet like Pilgrim Fathers in silver lamé breeches, still they come.

No breeches more silvery than Gary's. Back home, in the land he and his sherbet-sucking fans may well call Glittertannia, where it isn't unusual to find teen magazines running contests to find him his ideal wife – mouth, preferably 'kissable'; eyes, 'must be two of them'; age, 'better not to be over 30' – he's never had one single land outside the Top 4. Over here, Gary's only made the Top 10 once, which is why he's finally making his maiden coast-to-coast US press junket of promotional parties in the hairy-chested hope 'I Love You Love Me Love' will make it twice. The last gathering of cocktails and cameras being in New York, where after an hour or so grinning like a ventriloquist's dummy to a roomful of freeloading strangers who wouldn't know him from Freddie Starr he makes his sheepish excuses and glitters off into the night.

Mere minutes before a late-running Marc arrives. A chubbier Marc since he last bounced in the back of a yellow cab over Manhattan potholes. So chubby anyone who never physically saw Gary leave might consider the outside chance Marc's just scoffed him whole. A head-to-toe black blob in an oily PVC jacket, black cotton T-shirt, a leopard print headband poking through black curly hair and black plastic sunglasses shielding eyes black enough to have been burned into his flesh with a sooty poker. Eyes that roam with aloof disinterest, half expecting to find poor Gary still here. Definitely not expecting to find . . .

No! *Is it?*

The sunglasses come off. Their eyes meet, bump, then lock together like jigsaw pieces. And in that first dilation of the pupils, the first beat of recognition, everyone and everything else fades from view. No time, no space, just the two of them.

Because it's always *been* just the two of them.

And before either's mouth dares make a sound, in the slimmest splinter of a second, their faces telegraph a thousand ceasefires —

— *Soooo! Here we are, then.*

— Here we are!

— *Butch and Sundance.*

— The two who started it all.

— *Ah, now, c'mon! I started it, dear!*

— True. Even when jealousy was burning my guts like a burst appendix, I always knew. You were always the first.

— *And where I trod, you followed in my platform footsteps.*

— And walked further and climbed higher.

— *And then it was my turn to drown in my bile cursing your every magazine cover.*

— But by then I understood. When the crown was passed, when I felt its weight.

— *Because we're the only ones who've worn it.*

— The *only* ones.

— *You and I have walked through fire.*

— And neither of us got burned.

— *No?*

— OK. Maybe a little singed.

— *Your marriage?*

— Fucked, I think. Yours?

— *Same. What about, y'know, 'upstairs'?*

— The head? Oh, I'm off me fucking gourd, mate.

— *What we've been through, how can we not be?*

— But was all this really worth it?

— *Yes. No. Do we have any choice?*

— Yes. No.

— *Someone had to be me. Someone had to be you.*

— Lucky for the universe it was us.

— *And not Gary?*

— Ha! You always *were* a cheeky cunt.

— *And that's why you love me.*

— Yes, I do. Don't I?

— *Of course! You think I'm a groove.*

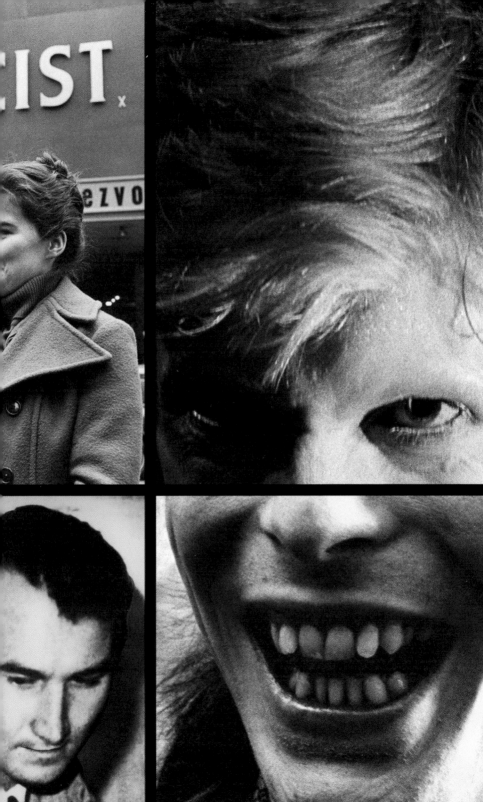

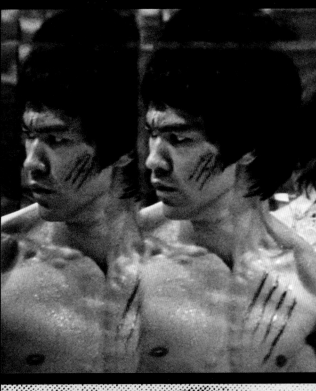
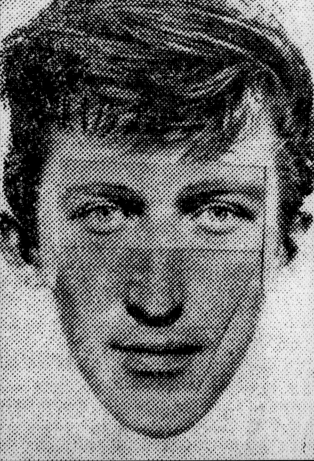

– And what about me?

– *What about you?*

– Do you . . . ?

– *Oh, don't make me say it. You know what I think.*

– Yes. I read your interviews.

– *And I read yours. Takes a bitch to know one, dear!*

– But you know I never meant a word of it.

– *And why would I ever want to bring you down?*

– Like brothers, then?

– *Cosmic twins. The Romulus and Remus who founded the empire. Except what I have, you haven't got.*

– And what you haven't got, I've enough for both of us.

– *You could be me if you tried. I could be you if I wanted to.*

– But you don't, and I don't.

– *Because you need me to be me so you can be you.*

– Which is why no one can touch us.

– *You know it, baby!*

– The two who started it all.

– *Just try to get rid of us!*

– So?

– *So?*

– So, what happens now?

– *Suppose one of us had better speak.*

– Shall we? OK.

– *OK?*

– Go on, then.

– *You first.*

– Marc . . .

– *Uh-uh. Out loud.*

'Marc . . .'

And though his smile beats him to it, David says it anyway.

'. . . My god, it's good to see you.'

TEN

BERNADETTE WAKES.

Not slowly, not groggily, but like a surge of electricity shocking her to consciousness. Bernadette wakes with a joy that the muscles in her face can't cope with. Bernadette wakes, and in the glow through her bedroom curtains sees the first rays of sunshine of the greatest day of her life.

Sunday, 26 May 1974.

Six a.m., Bernadette rises, washes and dresses in the clothes she laid out last night with bridal precision. Three-inch platform heels, black Oxford bags, her best floral blouse and her little black cardigan. With the same care she sits in front of her make-up mirror and gives her imperfections the fight of their life. *I know I am not beautiful but I will try and be as beautiful as I can for HIM.* Constant glances at his reflection on the wall over her shoulder, his face making her cheeks fizz even as she brushes them. She softly hums and softly sings and just as softly speaks. Private words between Bernadette and David and nobody's business but theirs.

The ticket that's been lying out on her dressing table all night she tucks in her purse, zipping and unzipping it to make sure it's definitely there before popping it inside her bag with a lipstick, a compact, her £10 camera and spare flashes. She is *almost* ready.

But Bernadette is a girl conditioned by 14 years of sacrament and ritual. She cannot simply leave her bedroom as she would any other day because today is not any other day. Today is The Day and ceremonies must be observed.

Do you renounce Satan and all his works and all his empty show?

She gathers up all his records and one by one lays them on top of her bed, directly below his posters.

Do you believe in God, the Father almighty, creator of Heaven and Earth?

She carefully arranges them.

Do you believe in Jesus Christ, His only Son, our Lord, who was born of the Virgin Mary, suffered death and was buried, rose again from the dead, and is seated at the right hand of the Father?

Pride of place, just at the bottom, the folder with her felt-tipped hand-lettered cover containing her unfinished English essay about the life, music and loves of an American superstar.

Do you believe in David Bruce Cassidy, 'Darling David', 'Superpuppy', that dreams are nuthin' more than wishes, that life is much too beautiful to live it all alone?

'I do! I do! I do! I do!'

When she gets home tonight all this, all these Davids – on her bed, on her wall, the ones rolled up on top of her wardrobe because she hasn't the space – will be waiting for her like a warm embrace.

When I get home tonight I will have seen him with my own eyes.

When she gets home tonight her camera roll will be full and her heart even fuller.

When I get home tonight I will be the happiest girl on God's Earth.

When she gets home tonight.

A last look at her bedspread shrine. She blows a kiss and quickly closes the door behind her, trapping it inside like a tiny bird.

A bite of toast and a slurp of tea. Her mum fussing around the kitchen as Bernadette prepares a packed lunch. Cucumber sandwiches, just like the ones the *Mirror* said David ate in a Hatton Garden snack bar on Friday. David is a vegetarian. Bernadette is trying.

The wall clock says 6.30 a.m. Over thirteen hours before David is due on stage, but Bernadette has a promise to keep, to her mum, to her dad, to God, and to His Son, our Lord. She is a good Catholic girl and every good Catholic girl must go to Mass. Right on time, the doorbell rings. Her best friends, Vanda and Margaret, all good Catholic girls together, dolled up for David but, just like Bernadette, none too tarty for Father O'Brien. Her mum in her best twinset, her dad in a shirt and tie, housekeys jingling. *Clunk!* And the Whelan household is silent as a tomb.

Early morning service, St George's Cathedral. The opening hymn, 'Holy God, We Praise Thy Name'. Sandwiched between her friends and her mum and dad, Bernadette lost in a trance. *Holy God, please hurry up!* One hour feels like ten. The constant ups and downs, the readings, the creed, the shaking hands.

'Peace be with you.'

'And also with you.'

The body of Christ. Bernadette waits her turn to receive it with cupped hands before popping the wafer on her tongue, trying not to swallow too quickly as she walks back up the aisle with a mouthful of Jesus.

Do this in memory of me.

And her headful of David.

I find myself alone with only memories of you.

But she is a good girl and has said her prayers, and if there's a God in Heaven, He will have heard them. And He shall deliver her from evil.

'Thanks be to God!'

The three girls fly out of the cathedral like racing pigeons. On the pavement, a clutched hand and a mother's goodbye. 'You be careful,' she says, the light winking off the Jesus round her neck. 'We will!' Bernadette waves and smiles, all sins absolved. *Peace be with you.* Six teenage feet gallop across the road, and in another minute her daughter slips out of her sight.

The Tube station as deserted as any other rushless Sunday morning. Nothing open but newsagents, and if only Bernadette knew, she'd stop to buy today's *People* with its photo of her David meeting two handicapped fans in the BBC canteen. But just gone 8 a.m. they're already northwards on the Bakerloo, laughing like the Smash robots, delirious by the time they change at Oxford Circus. There are others just like them milling along the platform. They don't need to read the name on their patches and T-shirts. They can tell by the faces. 'Sugar Baby Love' by the Rubettes is this week's number 1, and even though David Cassidy didn't sing it, girls like this are the reason it got there. Their eyes spill with it. Belief in a world of pop and romance and loving your baby love because you don't want to make them blue. Even as they sit rattling on a dirty grey carriage with faded seats and peeling advertising that smells of stale smoke and mop buckets, life is sweeter than a packet of Fruit Pastilles. If you placed a stethoscope to any of their chests, all you would hear is *bop-shoo-waddys* and a soaring *ahhh-ahhh*. Because, in May 1974, this is what little girls are made of. Lipsmackin' Pepsi and Sugar Baby Love.

The train pulls in to the platform and out they *bop-shoo-waddy*, up the escalator and into the *ahhh-ahhh* of the morning sunshine. Only a short *bop-shoo-waddy* up the road and a mighty *ahhh-ahhh* at the first glimpse of White City Stadium. Bernadette catches her breath.

They are not the first. Of course they're not the first. The first were here last night, sleeping in cars so they could paste themselves up against the gates while Bernadette was still brushing her teeth. There must be three or four hundred here already. Now three or four hundred and three.

Nine a.m. All that stands between Bernadette and her David is eleven hours of waiting. Like the longest Mass of her life, but with better hymns as the line becomes a scarf-waving choir breaking out in choruses of 'Daydreamer' and 'Cherish'. The three girls sing along, shiny faces and airy voices. The queue grows and the sky above clouds over an even grey. White with a pale but visible stain of bubbling darkness.

Excitement smothers hunger, but when Bernadette can't fight it anymore she sits and pecks at a cucumber sandwich. Her friends peck at their own, and between them they share a bag of cheese and onion crisps. They talk about David and David and David. Bernadette missed him on yesterday's *Saturday Scene* with Sally James because she was at work, but they all saw the pictures in the papers of him at the Radio Luxembourg studios on Friday, waving to fans from the balcony in his aviator shades and John Jay College of Criminal Justice T-shirt. They squeak and 'aw!' and wipe the crumbs from their lips, wondering if he's serious about all the things he's been saying in the papers these past few weeks since he announced he was quitting. About hating *The Partridge Family* and wanting to 'live an ordinary life again', about this tour really being 'goodbye to the kids' because he wants his fans 'to be in no doubt that I really mean it – that this really is the end of it all'.

And then commotion. Surging, screaming commotion.

The stadium gates. They weren't due to open till six, but by four the teenage refugee camp along Wood Lane commands action be taken.

Thirty-five thousand tickets have been sold with another five thousand available today in an effort to beat the touts. Forty thousand tickets. And not one with a specified seating allocation.

The gaping metal jaws swing open wide as a whale and in pour the plankton, a crazed stampede that wouldn't be any crazier if they were fleeing gunfire. Hair flying, ankles wobbling, bag straps slipping, trousers flapping, faces flushing, armpits sweating, mascara running, pelting, pelting, pelting towards the stage that's been erected at the far end of the grassy oblong surrounded by its famous dog track. Nothing in their way. No stewards, no policemen, no fences, no break barriers. Just empty space begging to be occupied, first come, first squashed. And there in the centre of the charge, Bernadette and her friends sprinting for their lives. *Come on! You can do it! Faster, faster! Closer, closer! Come on, come on! Nearly! Nearly! Nearly! Keep going! Keep going! You can do it! You can do it! That's it! YEEEESSS!*

They stop, purple-faced, panting furiously, lungs aching, wiping the damp hair from their foreheads. There must be at least ten, maybe fifteen rows in front between them and the barrier. Then another twenty feet after that to the stage. But they're close enough. Bernadette's heart thumps. *When I get home tonight I will have seen him with my own eyes. When I get home tonight I will be the happiest girl on God's Earth.* Behind her, thousands more, stretching all the way to the back and flooding the stands on each side. Bernadette checks her watch.

Only four more hours to go.

DEHYDRATING, THREE TO TWO TO ONE. Already boiled dry as Radio 1's Tony Blackburn appears to stray shrieks, here to set the mood and spin the hits, and what better than the number 1 sound of 'Sugar Baby Love'. But you can hardly hear the Rubettes for the natives' roar.

'WE WANT DAVID!'

The grey sky above, the darkness within, the anticipation below.

Ahhh-ahhh!

Bernadette, hot, nervous, excited, uncertain, just about holding her ground. All around her, waving scarves, shaking rosettes, singing, shouting, beetroot faces hot with tears, and the first blurs of limp bodies being dragged out by stewards over the barrier.

'WE WANT DAVID!'

Then human movement on stage.

'WE WANT DAVID!'

Then animal screaming.

'WE WANT DAVID!'

Then a false alarm.

It's not David. It's the support band. Sixteen drainpiped legs of manly *bop-shoo-waddy* from Leicester, all dressed like teddy bear Teddy Boys in blinding white brothel creepers and primary colour drape jackets bright as untouched strips of plasticine. Six months ago, this was the group who were offered, and refused, first dibs on the song the Rubettes have since taken to number 1. They chose instead their own knuckle-dusted 'Hey Rock And Roll', currently thumping in triplets up the charts to this week's Top 10. Enough kids know it to excitably chant along and half an hour of knock-kneed bonymaronying proves just enough for Showaddywaddy not to outstay their welcome. But the light is fading, and the body count backstage is growing fast. Twenty, thirty, forty girls, half alive and horizontal.

'WE WANT DAVID!'

The moment so close, the tension unbearable. All Bernadette, all any girl can think is he must already be *here*, somewhere in the stadium, backstage getting ready to go on. They smell him like a distant kill on a Serengeti downwind.

'WE WANT DAVID!'

The heat of so many bodies so close together, chests flattening into spines and arms pinning against arms, and everyone swaying no, no, no not this way, no, no, no not that way. The stewards just standing and staring, bemused and amused, like trawlermen gawping at their netted catch.

'WE WANT DAVID!'

Bernadette, gasping, struggling to reach into her bag to check her camera.

When I get home tonight . . .

But home suddenly feels very far away. Home is her bedroom and David on her walls and the sound of his voice on her record player and his fan club notepaper with 'I think I love you' and her unfinished school essay about the life, music and loves of 'David Cassidy, Superstar!'

When . . . I . . . get . . . home . . . tonight . . .

Home she isn't scared. Home she isn't wishing she was somewhere else. Home she isn't deafened by wailing panic. Home she can move. Home she can breathe.

. . . h-h-h-help . . .

But she can't. Move or breathe or barely see, not the flash of lightning, not the billowing plume of smoke from a flare canister, not the hazy figure emerging out of the mist, feet first, kicking his legs in time to the jerking vaudeville melody of 'The Puppy Song'. Behind her, Vanda and Margaret clawing at her shoulder, trying to pull her back, Margaret losing first her footing, then her shoes, but Bernadette keeps on falling forward, further out of reach, her bag slipping off her shoulder, further towards the superstar with the scarlet tail suit and cane she can't even see.

. . . n-n-no . . . oh . . . D-D-David . . . no . . .

Bernadette, not a person anymore, just part of a lava flow destroying everything in its path, girl swallowing girl swallowing girl, vicious with the molten heat from a billion magazine covers, a billion double-page pin-ups, a billion fact files, a billion lies about the scared young man on stage looking out across a mass teenage recreation of Rubens' *Fall of the Damned* kidding himself that this is only rock'n'roll, not genocide.

. . . oh . . . G-G-God . . .

And the stewards, panicking, sweating, some stripped to the waist, tugging at the limbs flailing in the teenage quicksand.

. . . h-help . . . me . . . Jeees-sus . . .

And so many suffocating bodies they're running out of stretchers.

. . . p-p-plee-ee-ase . . .

And the music stops as a fuzzy voice starts to yell 'MOVE BACK! PLEASE MOVE BACK!'

. . . our F-Father who-o-o . . . a-a-art . . .

And every second without respite the non-stop screaming. Horrible, *horrible* screaming. Joan of Arc burned at the stake screaming. The National Guard opening fire on Kent State University students screaming. Turkish Airlines Flight 981 crashing into a forest outside Paris killing everyone on board screaming. Until, as the concert is halted and the stage empties, as girls faint and vomit and beg for help like weak slippery seal pups writhing over one another, cut and bruised and weeping and choking, in an appeal for calm someone decides to play a record over the PA.

. . . oh . . . Mum.

And that record is by the Wombles.

'*Underground, overground . . .*'

Maybe the last music Bernadette ever hears. Because when they finally fish out her trampled sagging body, she has no pulse.

Bernadette isn't breathing.

All those Masses. All those Our Fathers. All those confirmation vows. All that renunciation of Satan and all his works and his empty show. All that belief in the Father almighty and creator of Heaven and Earth and Jesus Christ His only Son. All those hymns. All those communions. All those confessions. All those Christmases. All those Easters. All those Lents. All those scriptures at school and the nuns who shook them into her. All that youth. All that innocence. All that love. All that future. All the husband and kids and grandkids to be. All that joy. All that life. All those times she humbly begged her God to deliver her from evil. That same God, deaf. His Bernadette, dead.

'CHRIST, GET HER TO AN AMBULANCE!'

Dead. On a stretcher behind the stage, with her best blouse torn to rags, her tummy bare, her little white bra exposed, her arms drooped over the sides, her head in the hands of an ambulanceman named Terry, his face enclosed around hers in a frantic kiss of life while the Wombles sing about wombling free and newsmen who know a front-page drama when they see one pop flash bulbs around her head.

Dead. As Terry keeps pumping at her chest to massage her heart, as the sirens wail the few yards round the corner to Hammersmith Hospital, as they rush her into the emergency room, as her clothes are cut away and tubes shoved down her throat, as her mum and dad sit at home in Stockwell watching the telly, as her essay for school lies unfinished beside all the records on her bed.

Dead. As the stadium stewards chuck water and empty Coke cans at the front rows thinking it will make the crush retreat, as an American reporter from the *NME* named Chrissie Hynde wriggles free from the chaos in disgust, as David Cassidy returns to the stage 20 minutes later in a pair of dungarees and starts wriggling his bum to the screams of thousands upon thousands of the not-yet-dead.

Dead. Until the *beep!* and hum of an artificial respirator.

'She's got a heartbeat!'

She. *She?*

And nobody even knows her name.

TWENTY-FOUR HOURS LATER, THEY DO. Margaret, minus her shoes, and Vanda join the hundreds who've missed their last train home besieging Shepherd's Bush police station in the hope they'll find her. But even before they identify her lying in intensive care, images of Bernadette on a stretcher, her blouse ripped and bra showing as Terry the ambulanceman gives her the kiss of life are already rolling off the press. Even before anyone informs her mum and dad, not sleeping well, wondering why Bernadette never came home, why she hasn't rung to tell them where she is, photographs of their unresponsive pulseless daughter are being printed on the front covers of the *Mirror* and the *Express*. Even before a telephone rings in Crowhurst House and a receiver trembles at the words 'Mrs Whelan? I'm calling from Hammersmith Hospital . . .' there are strangers reading about an unnamed '*teenage girl casualty*' and '*heart-failure girl*' beside pictures of Bernadette headlined 'TEENYMANIA' and '700 CASSIDY GIRLS HURT'. Even before her father is handed what's left of his daughter's blouse, now a shredded bloodstained rag, Bernadette is famous.

'CASSIDY GIRL BERNADETTE FIGHTS FOR LIFE'.

Monday teatime, named on the cover of the *Evening News* next to her Notre Dame school portrait: hair all licked down in a centre parting, smiling sheepishly with no make-up, a photo any schoolgirl would hate because it makes her look like a child. A silly, goofy child. But that's not the Bernadette who went to White City. That Bernadette wore eye shadow, blusher, lipstick and earrings, looking as most 14-year-old girls try to look, about 17. Like she looks in the Woolies' photobooth pics that eventually turn up in Tuesday's tabloids. The morning after her parents have been told to prepare for the worst.

Bernadette has inoperable brain damage. By the time she was rescued and her heart restarted, the oxygen supply to her head had been cut off for too long. In the unlikely event she wakes from her coma, the doctors are afraid to say, their daughter will almost certainly be . . .

A vegetable?

'God, spare her!'

In Bernadette's bedroom, her parents perch on the edge of her bed for photographers, careful not to disturb her display of David Cassidy records exactly as she left it, exactly as they vow to leave it until the day she comes home. Mr Whelan, Peter, looks emotionally absent. A body waiting for its mind to arrive. Mrs Whelan, Bridget, looks hollowed out. There is nothing inside Bridget Whelan. Her eyes, black windows to a tortured abyss. Everything that ever was Bridget Whelan has been scooped out, leaving just an empty shell howling with pain like a storm trapped inside a jar. She still has her Jesus round her neck because she's still trying to understand, even as the darkness flattens her like a car crusher, even as her universe grows ever more bitterly godless with her every stifled inhalation. Until the moment of surrender.

'Oh . . . God!'

Her mute husband's arm grips her shoulder.

'*Why* did this have to happen?'

The same question is asked of the concert promoter. His name is Mel Bush, the same Mel Bush who last year promoted David Bowie's *Aladdin Sane* tour. The papers want to know whether he accepts any responsibility for what happened at White City.

This is what he tells them.

'These girls sleep, eat and dream David Cassidy for three months before he gets here. When he appears on stage they just crumble. There were 35,000 at the show and I would say 34,998 of them enjoyed themselves. They've had their scream, their shout, their faint. It was good exercise for them.'

Good exercise for Bernadette, a mask over her face as the respirator pumps air into her weakening lungs. Beside her bed, a man dressed in black makes the sign of the cross with his right hand, a fat leather book in his left. He speaks a little louder than a whisper in a low sombre voice.

'Eternal rest grant unto her, O Lord, and let perpetual light shine upon her. May she rest in peace. Amen. May almighty God bless us with His peace and strength, the Father and the Son and the Holy Spirit.'

Behind the priest, cards from well-wishers, strangers, young David Cassidy fans just like her, and a giant bouquet in a vase and – oh, Bernadette! If only you could wake up and read what it says on these flowers!

'*Please get well soon. Best wishes and love, David Cassidy.*'

He knows who she is. Of course he knows. Her picture and his have been side by side in every paper since Monday morning. He's cancelled radio and TV interviews because of her. He even held a special press conference where he said, 'I hope to God that she makes it.' Hear that, Bernadette? He wants you to make it, wants you to *live*.

Beep! Beep! Beep!

Because if she lives, then none of this will be his fault. That's what he keeps telling himself. *Not my fault.* That's what everyone around him keeps telling him. *Not your fault.* That's why they lied to him, why they told him she's in intensive care because of a pre-existing heart condition, that in the excitement of seeing him she suffered a cardiac arrest. So it will never be his fault. So he believes whatever bullshit they need him to believe so he doesn't chicken out of his last scheduled show at Manchester's Maine Road stadium, where only half the allocated 18,000 crowd show up because the White City headlines scared the other half away. So he'll make it all the way to his very last encore, a one-off special rendition of a Bob Dylan song.

'It's All Over Now, Baby Blue'.

Almost over now, baby Bernadette. As the daily news stories become smaller and sadder, like a novel where everybody's guessed the ending and just wants to get it over and done with.

Wednesday. Another nine-hour vigil, her mum no longer able to walk from the hospital unassisted, her dad just about able to speak to the *Express*.

'All that is left for us to do is to pray for a miracle.'

And so they pray. And the worst of it is Bernadette can't speak. Can't tell them they're wasting their time. Can't tell them He's not listening. Because now she knows. He's not there. But all she can do is *beep!* And all they can do is pray. And plead, and mumble, and moan, and beg, and squeeze their rosaries so hard they could pop like grapes. Until early Thursday morning, in the darkness before dawn. When her life support is switched off.

When the praying stops.

★

'CLUMSY CLOGS CLUE TO KILLER PILE-UP'.

Dead but not yet in her grave, they try to blame Bernadette's shoes.

'I am going to ask witnesses who were actually there on the floor,' declares the coroner, opening the inquest. 'Most of them are young girls. A large number of these people wear platform shoes. As soon as there is movement in the crowd there is a tendency to fall. This is not an inquiry into footwear, but this factor must be considered.'

Shoes. Not the promoter, not the wrong choice of venue, not the Greater London Council who refused permission for screens to be erected to project closed-circuit TV of the gig so everyone in the stadium could see properly, not the penned-in conditions which had those who survived calling it 'the suicide gig', not the overrun St John's Ambulance crews who said they've 'never seen anything like this at a pop concert', not the stage security, not the stewards, not the police, not anyone who will ever be made to stand trial for any negligence which may have contributed to her death. Just silly girls in their silly shoes trying to get close to their silly pop stars.

Case closed. Tight as her coffin.

Her neighbours pack the landing of Crowhurst House to see the hearse. Young, old, black, white, mothers, fathers, teens, toddlers, gazing down, trying their best to connect shining chrome and a flower arch on a car rack with the smiling girl in the school uniform they used to know. Hundreds more pupils from the same school wait round the corner at Our Lady of the Rosary on Brixton Road. Girls who came back after half-term on Monday to an empty desk in the classroom and a look on the nuns' faces they've never seen before. A look of barely concealed fear that they've run out of answers before any questions have been asked. Because there aren't any answers. There is just a gaping wound of sorrow whose bleeding no scriptures can stem.

The final journey to the cemetery, the cortege rolls slowly down Brixton Hill, past newsstands announcing: 'JACKSON 5 SCRAP POP TOUR OVER RIOT FEAR'. At the last minute, the Jacksons have cancelled their upcoming UK dates, due to begin next week, as a direct result of White City. From the back seat of their car, her mum and dad read the headlines.

Something good has come out of this. Dear God. Something good.

The uncaring sun shines and a soft breeze jingles the leaves of the nearby poplar tree as her casket is lowered in a grassy southern corner near the footpath. A new plot with no neighbours: for now, just Bernadette, alone. A small huddle of her friends stare at the dozen wreaths lying atop the fresh soil. One of them is shaped like a guitar. The friends clutch one another, dabbing their eyes, failing to find sense in a world that's stopped making any, every last grain of Sugar Baby Love savagely beaten from their bodies.

But a million others overflow with it, still. Beyond the cemetery gates, a million more Bernadettes. Still living, still breathing, still senselessly in love with the face on the bedroom wall. Some unsure whether to swap David Cassidy for the mince'n'tatty complexions of the Bay City Rollers. Some faithfully swooning over David Essex. Some sat cross-legged beneath their floor-to-ceiling altar to David Bowie, high on the spiritual enlightenment of *Diamond Dogs* – his new album, his new sermon, his ten new commandments, released the day after Bernadette died in hospital. Already at number 1 on the day she's buried. A record she will never hear.

Just as she'll never hear her parents crying every time they visit her graveside. Or her friends when they come and sob along to 'Could It Be Forever' on a battery cassette player. Or the whistling of the wind around her headstone. Or the birds in spring or the thunder storms in winter. Because for her, the music is over. The record has ended. The only sound is silence.

Peace be with you.

Bernadette stops.

ELEVEN

THE SHOW MUST GO ON. Duke Ellington dies and Rick Wakeman quits Yes, but the show must go on. Derek from the Rollers collapses with exhaustion and the son of Hattie Jacques leaves the Wombles after being arrested for cannabis possession, but the show must go on. A theatre burns down, nearly taking Southend pier with it during the filming of Ken Russell's *Tommy*, and Leo Sayer, who only became famous by dressing like a clown and singing 'The Show Must Go On', now decides he no longer wants to dress like a clown. But, even for Leo, the show must go on. Because the show always goes on.

The Show.

You couldn't call it anything else. Certainly not a gig, not even a concert. More a production, a Ziegfeld folly, a Broadway Melody of 1974. Even if the ads call it 'The Year of the Diamond Dogs' anyone who can afford a ticket – and at seven to ten dollars, brother, they ain't cheap – won't be left in any doubt what they've witnessed. This is The David Bowie Show.

Opening on a Friday night in Montreal, between *Serpico* down in Westmount Square and *The Exorcist* up at Loew's, in an almost-but-not-quite-full ice hockey arena. An electronic scoreboard hangs down over the centre of the rink where not two months ago the local Canadiens lost 2–3 to the New York Rangers in the playoffs. But tonight the scoreboard

is off, the rink covered with row upon aisled row of chairs facing a
raised platform where the exposed Hunger City set waits like a deserted
Disneyland attraction to greet the thousands almost-but-not-quite-filling
it out. The same longhairs, skinny T-shirts and faded denims smelling
of Labatt's 50 and marijuana who were here for Floyd and Crimson,
punctuated by shinier clusters of lightning-faced zealots, some already
batting violet eyelids over the programme robbing everyone who reads
it the anticipatory thrill of not knowing what songs will be played in
what order. All of them mentally measuring up the stage, trying to figure
out what's that blue splodge on that big wonky building, and is that
thing some sort of bridge, and why is the drumkit shoved away over
in the corner with the piano and the amplifiers almost out of sight, and
whether that's blood dripping *down* that skyscraper towards that big red
lump shaped like a female torso, or whether instead that's blood spurting
up that skyscraper from that big red lump which, on second glance, looks
more like a fat penis. And why there's no support act, just 45 minutes of
sound effects pumping through the speakers – jungle noises, sex moans,
tolling bells, computer squeaks, rain, thunder, bangs, crashes, guttural
demonic growls and a thumping heartbeat. Until the moment when the
house lights dim and an eerie wind howls over the level-testing plinks and
plucks of unseen musicians somewhere in the darkness. When The David
Bowie Show begins.

With spotlights dancing over the cityscape and the funky wocca-wocca
of '1984'. The crowd scream before they can see him, and if they knew
he was already there staring at them from deep in the shadows, they'd
scream even louder. They do when they hear his voice, still invisible as
he sings the first verse. Louder still, come the chorus, when a circle of
light picks him out like a search beam freezing on a convict by the prison
wall: leaning at the rear of the set in a cream suit, red braces over a blue
jumper with white dots, a silver chain hanging from waist to right trouser
pocket, yellow socks and red shoes; his hair, an electric ginger, brushed in
a soft feathery fringe and trimmed at the back. In an instant embarrassing
every Ziggy clone here.

Then dancers. Two of them, men in braces and spats, his old friend
Geoff and another named Gui, officially listed as the 'Dogs', sidling up to
David, jerking through the routines they've been rehearsing for the past

few weeks with Toni Basil, the hip choreographer behind street dance troupe the Lockers. Together they strut and mince straight into 'Rebel Rebel', David swivelling his mic stand left to right, yet to smile or say 'good evening' or betray any acknowledgement the crowd even exist. Because he isn't here to interact. He is here to show off, then fuck off.

Whereas the band, here to clock on and clock off, are squashed over in the corner under the building with the yellow blob. The only threat to their silhouetted anonymity comes in 'Moonage Daydream' when the guitar player is given licence to stretch the chain of his kennel and whine on his fretboard. Those who bother to read their programme will learn his name is 'Earl Slick': those who bother to read his birth certificate will learn it's Frankie. But once his solo is over, the chain yanks and back he cowers, his purpose served to kill enough time so David can climb to the bridge between the set's two main towers and await his next reveal.

Basking in the yellow glow of mock streetlamps, a trench coat over his shoulders and a smoking cigarette in his hand, looking like the moody Sinatra of *No One Cares* and sounding not so dissimilar as he whips the Vegas out of 'Sweet Thing'. The bridge slowly descends, the coat comes off, the sleeves roll up and David slides upstage as the songs topple like dominoes one straight on top of the other. 'Changes', cocktailing into 'Suffragette City', whambamming into a brassy Latin arrangement of 'Aladdin Sane' as David shuffles like a geisha holding a face mask on a stick, its lightning flash echoed by the giant zigzag illuminating one of the city blocks behind him. Broadwaying into a slow gospel 'All The Young Dudes', boogalooing into a sassy jazzy 'Cracked Actor', David perching on a stool in sunglasses and cape as he serenades a skull, Hamlet to Yorick, surrounded by Hollywood baby spots, the Dogs playing paparazzi and powderpuffing his cheeks. Tinseltowning into 'Rock 'N' Roll With Me', the fourth wall finally collapsing for just a few seconds when a girl hurtles to the edge of the stage with a bouquet of flowers. David takes them, kissing her on the lips. The song ends. The city plunges into darkness.

End of Act One.

WITH A BANG, ACT TWO. Humping his mic stand to a raucous 'Watch That Man', then slouching into a painfully literal 'Drive-In Saturday',

David swiping at a 12-string guitar as his Dogs dumbly chew popcorn pretending to watch a movie. With the last strum he vanishes again amid a chaos of piano runs, the stage drowning in blue, twinkling with sputtering starlight. The fans who can spot a tune in a couple of chords are cheering even before he reappears sat in a window at the top of the bloody tower with a red telephone in his hand. The fans who can't soon join them when he pulls the receiver to his lips and 'Space Oddity' lifts off. So does David. Floating out up above the audience, seemingly by magic for the time it takes anyone to realise his chair is on the arm of a hydraulic catapult. As he sings about the wife he loves very much his eyes steal a secret glance at the front row. There's Angie, in the same 'Can Can' dress she wore in a recent fashion shoot for *The Sun*. Her smile crackles back up at him. If only for the show's sake, yes. *She knows*. And somewhere in the darkness, a few seats down, someone else's stomach lurches efficiently.

The chair floats back into the tower with Major Tom slumped dead but the voice of David loud and alive. The record of 'Future Legend' fills another short scene change before he's back on the bridge for 'Diamond Dogs' with a coil of thin rope in his hand. As he's lowered to the stage its ends are taken up by his two snarling Dogs primed for a dramatic tug of war, ending with David trussed up and helpless as a lassoed stallion but never missing a note. Untangling him, the Dogs stretch the rope out to form a makeshift boxing ring. David's bodyguard, Stuey, appears dressed in a trainer's tracksuit, strapping him into gloves so his mic rests in the gap between thumb and mitt. And for the next three minutes, sparring thin air, 'Panic In Detroit' becomes a daft pugilist pantomime ending in a K.O.

The plot thins and the confusion thickens when a large oblong mirrored vehicle crawls upon the stage, a bit taller than a phone box, shaped something like a giant diamond, David, at first, perched on top of it for 'Big Brother'. Then with the stuttering climax of 'Chant Of The Ever Circling Family' he suddenly slips inside, hidden from view until its sides split open and a giant black hand sparkling with yellow bulbs drops from the front exposing David safe in its blue-tubed womb singing 'Time'. He escapes by means of the staircase down its palm when the hand rises, the sides close up, the diamond rolls off and the Dogs roll back on to help him rip up a paper skyscraper during the mayhem of 'The Width

Of A Circle'. But for David the temptation of its squealing instrumental mayhem proves devilishly too long for his idle hands to resist: not for the first time in his career he reminds a paying audience why 'mime' is a four-letter word.

The squealing eventually stops, but the dumbshow doesn't, and whatever 'The Jean Genie' deserves it definitely isn't David and his Dogs mock fighting their way through a game of musical chairs. David is punched. David is raised above their heads. David's limp body is dumped back in his seat. And suddenly it's just David, alone, spotlights glaring from the foot of his stage casting his giant shadow against what's left of Hunger City for the grand finale of 'Rock 'N' Roll Suicide'. All sets now unnecessary, all crass props forgiven, all sins of mime redeemed. Just this song, that voice, this man.

Gimme your hands.

Ignoring all stewards, those who can storm forth and do. Then, pulling his hand free, David turns and swaggers to the back of the stage. Into the darkness.

Leaving behind an almost-but-not-quite-full ice hockey arena to imagine its own end credits. A giant flaming red widescreen 'THE END'. Or a Monty Python safety curtain 'PISS OFF'. Because no sooner do the house lights rise than a metallic voice cuts through the clapping, loud and sharp as a third period buzzer.

'David Bowie has left the theatre . . .'

THE SHOW, OF COURSE, GOES ON. To Ottawa, where the crowd start a riot when they realise there's no encore. To Toronto, where it begins with an announcement apologising for David's laryngitis and ends with Angie brawling with security for trying to keep the kids in their seats. Back across the US border to Ohio, where extreme heat in Toledo forces him off stage for 15 minutes while he receives oxygen. Through the Midwest, David's pose weakening a fraction as he starts slipping in a few 'good evening's and 'thank you's between the showing off and fucking off. Down into the South, deciding to scrap 'Drive-In Saturday' and the destruction of the paper tower. Deeper still into Florida, where a bee stings the lorry driver whose trailerful of Hunger City careers off the highway into mangroves crawling with rattlesnakes. That evening in Tampa, another special announcement.

'Ladies and gentlemen. The concert you're going to see tonight is not the show we had planned for you. Due to an unfortunate road accident, half of our stage scenery, costumes and lighting equipment is in a local swamp 15 miles north of here. There was talk of cancelling tonight's performance but David Bowie would not hear of it and insisted we go on.'

The show. It always does.

EVEN CHRISTINE'S. Weekday mornings at 9.30 a.m., live from a TV studio not 60 miles south from the Florida swamp which, were it not for tow ropes, would have swallowed Hunger City. The Sarasota housewives' after-breakfast choice either *Sesame Street*, old Lucille Ball reruns or current affairs with Chris and her *Suncoast Digest* on WXLT Channel 40.

She's been with the station over a year now, an attractive and intelligent 29-year-old host who her colleagues think of as 'the sparkplug' of the newsroom. Take this morning, the first day of a brand-new format for the show and Chris is here bright and early with her usual smile and a steaming Styrofoam cup of coffee. A few last-minute scribbled changes to her script and she's behind her desk, calm, fully prepared and ready for the red light.

'Good morning . . .'

Hers the voice and face broadcasting today's headlines out over the Gulf of Mexico. Local drug arrests by undercover police. An industrial dispute over refuse collection. And a restaurant robbery shootout that's been caught on camera. She reads the scripted introduction to the footage. Then a pause. Then something in her ear.

'Sorry,' she says, ever the professional. 'We seem to be having a problem with the tape.' And returns to the paper script in her hand.

'In keeping with Channel 40's policy of bringing you the latest in blood and guts in living colour, you are going to see another first . . .'

She pauses as her right hand reaches below her desk.

'. . . attempted suicide.'

Then bringing out a .38 revolver and pressing it tight to the back of her skull she pulls the trigger and blows her brains out.

The last image the viewers of WXLT see before the blackout of an emergency 'Technical Difficulties' card is the lifeless head of Christine Chubbuck smacking off her desk like a melon off a truck before dropping out of sight.

She leaves no explanatory note. Just her amended script, now spattered with blood, containing handwritten instructions for the next station news bulletin describing her death, a grieving mother out in Crescent Beach, unpaid psychiatrist bills and the unbearable guilt of her colleague Rob. Well, wasn't it only a week ago when he'd asked her why she'd recently purchased a gun? 'I had this really nifty idea,' laughed Chris, 'that I'd bring it to work and blow myself away during the show.'

The show. Because nothing else matters, only the show. Even if hers is over, tomorrow night on a stage in Boston, the city where Chris went to university, David will still be out there singing 'Rock 'N' Roll Suicide'.

It must go on.

AT LEAST TILL NEW YORK CITY. The last stop of the first leg. The big one.

Madison Square Garden.

Did any cigar taste so sweet as the thick stick of Cuban rock sucking in the mouth of Tony Defries as he shuts his eyes and casts his mind back two summers? A June night in 1972. Flying in from London with David, straight into a limo from JFK to Pennsylvania Plaza to watch the greatest of them all, Elvis Presley, live at the Garden. Always knowing one day it would be their turn. And, just two years later, it is.

'MAINMAN PRESENTS BOWIE AT THE GARDEN'.

Two nights, sold out, the crown passing from one King to another.

Glory, glory, hallelujah!

Defries opens his eyes, unclenches his teeth, withdraws it to exhale a victorious milky-white cloud, then plops it back in.

Nope. No cigar ever did.

The cloud thins before his eyes, and like a genie just emerged from its lamp there's David. Dancing in the Garden spotlight, singing the old Eddie Floyd soul stomper 'Knock On Wood', his one new addition to the set since the tour began five weeks ago. Defries takes another suck, blankly ogling the stage with thoughts similar to that of a billy goat forced to watch *Singin' in the Rain*. Lights and pizzazz and noise and gibberish. His opinion hasn't altered since he first saw the rehearsal six weeks ago when he realised exactly how all those tens upon tens of thousands of dollars snapping in his in-tray have been spent. Phallic splodges, papier-mâché, a crane that sometimes gets stuck, a winch that sometimes collapses, an oversized Christmas bauble on wheels and three bistro chairs. But then, naturally, it was *never* going to be about the *show*, was it? Colonel Tony has learned from the master.

Blue Hawaii? As bad a film as ever earned five million dollars.

Kissin' Cousins? A piece of crap grossing another three.

Harum Scarum? Pure horseshit but with a box office of two million just keep feeding that horse.

Because the scenery, the costume, the action isn't important. Only the star. Only the sell. The golden rule: if you wanna see Bowie, you gotta buy a ticket. And this weekend, he's sold 28,000.

Mmm-mmm! Sure is a fine cigar.

A whoop as the sad strains of 'Space Oddity' ring around the Garden and David emerges from on high, hovering above the rabble. Half-watching, half-listening, Defries's thoughts similarly drift.

So, then, Colonel Tony? You've sold out the Garden. And you've finally got a hit album in America with *Diamond Dogs*, this week at number 5 in the States, next week number 1 in Canada. What next?

He takes another satisfying puff. In his ear, a voice sings about circuits being dead and something wrong.

Is there? Nah. Not really. A few minor hiccups, maybe, but nothing so huge it can sink the battleship Mainman. Well, OK, so for all the good that Times Square billboard did, America has no more taken to Mick Ronson than it has silly old Jobriath. And no matter how many full-page press ads dedicated to her ballooning cleavage, nobody anywhere on the planet has taken to Dana Gillespie. And, yes, Amanda Lear can do as many UK tabloid spreads as she likes telling everyone she'll be starring in a Mainman film about the Russian underground comic-book heroine Octobriana with music especially written for her by David, but it's never going to happen. Same as the album he promised Wayne County and, besides, Wayne's just quit Mainman, same as his friends Leee and

Cherry, once the heart and soul of the New York office. Whereas the London office has been wound down entirely. And most of David's band are going to quit after the Garden, pissed off with Defries for trying to swindle them out of being paid for the live album they've just recorded in Philadelphia. And even the trailers carrying Hunger City wouldn't fit up the Garden's loading ramp, so the whole set had to be unpacked in the street and carried in a day in advance at greater expense. And while some reviews have been raves, others have *seriously* stunk. And this tour might bankrupt them yet. And that divorce from Mrs Defries just won't go away. And – *bleuch!* – suddenly this cigar doesn't taste quite as good as it did three sucks ago.

But, wait. Another suck, another puff and another milky-white cloud blooms in the air to the accompaniment of deafening cheers.

Ah! *That's* more like it. Because you know what that sound is? Receipts. Profits. *Money.* The sweet, sweet sound of the sell.

And, as the saying goes, the sell must go on . . .

ALL THE WAY TO THE GARDEN AFTERPARTY in a suite at the Plaza, just over the road from David's hotel where an elite guest list of forty Very Important People have been invited to drown themselves in champagne and flattery. Another tasty cigar for Colonel Tony as his head swivels like a gun turret, sucking and puffing from one face to the next. Some he knows, some he doesn't. Promoters, managers, company men like Clive Davis, actors, models and, unmistakably, the KGB-wary glower of the world's greatest dancer, Rudolf Nureyev, pinned up against the wall like he's warming his muscles to suddenly make a grand jeté over the salmon platter. And Angie, under the same civil ceiling as Ava and doing her polite best not to maim her with the nearest set of ice tongs. And Corinne, efficiently blending into the wallpaper. And Stuey, tight at David's hip, faithfully guarding the body of . . . *the star?*

The gun turret smiles and fires a smoke cloud.

Correction. The *product.*

And such a thin and bony product these days too. Look at him, embracing Mick who's just Jaggered in, falling into his arms like a bundle of firewood, the two of them twitching and teeheeing like guilty schoolboys. Then, in another puff of Defries's smoke, like an illusionist's trick, both suddenly vanish, the whole room straining the corner of its eye pretending not to notice or care where David and the singer of the Rolling Stones have got to.

'WHERE'S BOWIE?'

Except Bette Midler, molling in with a mouth that'd silence a Dodge City saloon. It's left to Angie, in plain view of everyone, to escort her through the open door of one of the bedrooms to a walk-in closet. Bette knocks, peers in, snorts, cackles, then barges inside, slamming the door behind her.

It's the best part of an hour before anyone sees her again. Or David, or Mick, all hiding inside, opening it for no one, not Angie, not Ava, not even Rudolf Nureyev who raps his besmirched Russian knuckles in vain.

Whereas outside the closet – ooh! – what *gossip* they make! A scandal as sweet as a spoiled cigar is bitter.

And both just as thick on the tongue the next morning.

TWELVE

UP, UP, UP INTO THE LIGHT. Dancing on the surface like a rippling blanket of diamonds. Breaking through with a soft splash to the dry heat of the scorching sun, droplets running off his body slick as rain down a windowpane. Blinking the water from his eyes, everything he can see is shimmering as if in a dream. The sun, the pool, the loungers, the glass with his drink and the chrome patio table where it rests. Like he has actually died and gone to heaven.

Except David Essex is alive and only gone to St Tropez.

It's not him that's dead. It's Jim. That's what this holiday is for now that he's finished filming *Stardust*. To cleanse himself of Jim MacLaine in a born-again ecstasy of good riddance to bad vibes. Scrub him from his mind and his body like an evil spirit, exorcised by chlorine and the Riviera sun.

David did a great job on Jim. He knows it. But there were times when Jim did a pretty good job on David too. The scenes when David really had to pull it out of himself – really had to *act* – and be as convincing a drug-binging paranoid megalomaniac rock monster as he could.

The awful things Jim made David do. Sex scenes. *Threesomes!* Live like a crazy recluse in a Spanish castle. Take a bath in his clothes. Punch Adam Faith. Poison a dog. Take an overdose. Commit suicide because he couldn't take the pressures anymore. The same pressures David lives with. Only, Christ, *what* a tragedy! That's all he could think filming those final scenes. *What a waste.*

But there are some roles you can't just walk away from. Some roles that won't let you. Characters are selfish bastards, and Jim MacLaine was as selfish a bastard as ever punched ink from a typewriter ribbon. So you have to be patient. Drown them one day at a time in a swimming pool in the South of France surrounded by the people you love. Your wife. Your little daughter.

Strum!

And your record plugger Steve.

The Jim MacLaine show is over, but David Essex must go on. His label want a new album by Christmas, which means writing new songs. Which means all this Côte d'Azur bliss is really just a working holiday after all.

David can't really complain. The sun, the pool, the rosé and the Roquefort. There are worse offices to do a day's graft, and so far the graft has been very promising. Especially the tune they came up with yesterday lunchtime, both sat drying off in their trunks, Steve twangling a few chords on guitar, the words popping into David's head with no more effort than squirting Ambre Solaire on his chest.

'*We're gonna make ya a star-ar-arrr!*'

They both think it sounds like a future number 1. And from the bottom of the pool, so does the sodden black phantom of Jim MacLaine. Still wet and not getting any dryer, looking up and laughing his scurvy laugh through the tiny twinkles on the surface to the bigger one sparkling around David's neck. A little silver star on a chain he's been wearing for months and grown so attached to, he can't take it off. But if he was gravely serious about casting out the devil of Jim MacLaine you really think he would have by now.

Why else would David Essex still be wearing the bastard's necklace?

THIRTEEN

'**MIRROR, MIRROR ON THE WALL**, who's the greatest of them all?'

Hello? Hello?

Ah! Of course, it's a French mirror, silly. Start again . . .

'**MIROIR, MIROIR, SUR LE MUR**, qui est le plus grand de tous?'

'Tu l'es, Marc!'

Like he needs a Parisienne looking glass to tell him. All the same.

'Mais oui, bien sûr! A champagne toast to you, Monsieur Miroir.'

He knocks back his flute in one gulp.

'Aah!'

Smacks his tongue. Twitches his lips. Pours himself another from the almost empty bottle. Bows his head to the surface of the coffee table. Sniffs violently. Jerks up, shaking his curls like a cheerleader's pom-pom. Screws up his nose. Wipes his eyes. Looks back over at the hotel mirror. Sees the little boy who bit the poisoned apple. Blinks. Sees the picture of Dorian Gray. Blinks again. Sees the greatest rock'n'roll star of them all. Smiles. Hears a telephone ring. Frowns. Then remembers.

Shit. Another interview.

Between the sipping and the sniffing and the blankly staring out of his window at the Eiffel Tower it's all Marc's been doing these past couple of days. Loafing in a penthouse suite in the Hilton dripfeeding his genius to the papers back home. He has a groovy new T. Rex single to promote,

'Light Of Love', which they won't play on *Top of the Pops* because *Top of the Pops* has been off air for weeks due to a BBC technicians' dispute. In pop's televisual vacuum 'She' by Charles Aznavour has since gargled its vinegary way to number 1 and like a striking French postal worker shall not be moved. The hardest hit are glam's walking dead: with nowhere to wiggle her leathers Suzi Quatro's latest misses the Top 10, and with the bitter irony of their best single The Sweet only just scrape it with their scarily brilliant 'The Six Teens'. Even David's 'Diamond Dogs' can't break the Top 20, meaning the odds have never been more stacked against Marc's favour. But he and Monsieur Miroir know different.

'I haven't slipped. Not in my chart. I'm still number 1. I won't go into all the faded star bit because I'm the one who created the elusive star. I leave it in the hands of the divine one and he's never let me down.'

The divine one, Dom Pérignon. Or maybe his sidekick, Dom Poudre de Nez.

'I'm stuck in a world which is crazy and I can't always do what I want to. I'm hardly ever in Britain these days but I have too many close links to quit. I have a flat and a house there – and a jukebox and a rocking horse! I could never sever my connections with them. It's heartbreaking not playing England. I love the M1 and fried egg and chips.'

The warm phone receiver in his hand, the bloated face in the mirror, the crystal echo of answers to questions that haven't been asked.

'I created Marc Bolan. Invented him if you like. And I really like being him. We live a crazy life together. I have no time for any of the things that many people consider to be important – things like a family, a home life, or even a normal relationship. It may seem sad to some people, but the truth is that to me, music comes before anything else. Without my music and my words, I could not exist . . . I suppose I'm a 26-year-old punk. But I am a musician. And a poet. And a success.'

And a hopeless fantasist.

'The only rival I've got is David Bowie . . .'

Or perhaps not?

'. . . and we're close friends.'

There, Marc. The truth at last.

'We spent some time together in New York before his American tour and spoke about this. We sorted out the future of rock trends for the next two years. We sat in my hotel suite and watched *A Clockwork Orange* ten times right through on closed-circuit television. That took us about three days.'

A truth halved.

'It reminded us both of our childhoods. People beating each other up and doing other nasty things. That was us. And I helped him find some of the musicians for his *Diamond Dogs* show. We worked on that a little bit together.'

Now slashed into quarters.

'. . . and one of the things we are planning is a film together. David will write the screenplay. I will write the music. And we will both appear in small roles. And direct it, together.'

And poor Monsieur Miroir so wants to laugh but daren't for fear of cracking.

'**MIRROR, MIRROR ON THE WALL,** who's the dumbest of them all?'

'You are, David.'

So fucking dumb the mirror's not even *on* the wall. It's flat on the table, dusty as a baker's bench with the flour you've just sucked up your nose through a rolled-up Benjamin so hard your eyes nearly shot out like a double-barrelled popgun. And staring back up at you through those smeared white specks, the skeletal death mask of the dumbest of them all. As you've only just found out.

How long has it taken you? Four whole years. See? Dumb!

Where did it all go so horribly wrong? How did you end up in this piteous mess? Think back, David. *Think* . . .

A memory fuzzes in his head like bad TV reception. A bang on the set top. The picture blinks, wobbles and settles.

A spring day in 1970. An office in Cavendish Square. God knows he thought it felt right at the time. So did Angie, sat there beside him, squeezing his hand as he wept with joy. The first time David met Tony Defries. *And he wept!*

But who's crying now? Ken Pitt, that's for sure. His old manager who clothed and fed and housed him, who took him on his arm to the theatre and the ballet, who encouraged him to act and 'mime', who bankrolled the film showcase that forced him to write his breakthrough hit, 'Space Oddity'. But that wasn't enough, was it? David wanted more and he wanted out but he didn't have the guts to tell Ken himself. So he went searching for an assassin and, boy, he found one. A real killer diller.

So Ken got whacked and he became Defries's boy. Or, to start with, Defries's and Laurence's boy. Dear old Laurence. He had the money Defries needed to spend on him, which he did. When no label would touch him, Laurence paid for studio time so he could make *Hunky Dory* and, thanks to him, and it, David got his deal with RCA. And how did he repay him? By getting Defries to whack Laurence too. That's David. As loyal as he is smart.

But that's when he made his big boo-boo. The one that's just taken a bite out of his ass so big he's barely a cheek left to sit on.

Mainman.

There's one born every minute, and the minute David signed on Defries's dotted line another prize model was spat out of the klutz factory. The kind who walked away as the ink dried believing he'd just been made an equal partner in his own management company. Straight down the line, everything fifty-fifty. Because that's what he and Defries had agreed.

That's what David assumed.

But who's got time to read the small print? Not David. Much too busy being magnificent, writing songs, making records, fucking anything that paints its own toenails, cramming more and more of that direful dum-dum dust up his snout.

Until the day comes.

When he pauses long enough between toots to wonder where exactly all the money, *his* money, has got to. Because here he is, just sold out two nights at Madison Square Garden, a Top 5 album in America, living in an ambassadorial suite in the Sherry, a limo on call, room service rich but other than the curly $100 bill still damp from his nostril, cash poor. With Defries nowhere to be seen, not even returning his calls. Out of reach, somewhere stretching his gums around another marrow-sized cigar, or forecasting the handsome profits of the next leg of David's tour, or costing more billboards for the next Mick Ronson album that won't sell, or licking his lips over Dana Gillespie's 44-inch bust, or ignoring the red invoices to pay Guy Peellaert for his *Diamond Dogs* artwork, or cancelling

Angie's company credit card, or picking out yet more furnishings for his penthouse, or putting another order in for several hundred dollars' worth of the finest Monte Cristos, or checking today's market price of gold bullion, or licking the cream from his fat cat whiskers while David hasn't so much as a foil bottle top to sniff.

Until the day comes.

Well, guess what, David? Today is punchline day.

Straight from the lips of his old friend, Zee, the last of the old *Pork* gang still working for Defries. Over a Pyrenees of gleepowder and a twilight-to-sunrise view across Central Park.

It takes a long time for Zee's punch to land. Many lines. Many grams. Mainly because David is seething, foaming, ranting – about Defries, about having no money, about being kept in the dark – but he isn't listening, like he's so bunged up with that dirt it's wadding his eardrums.

'Half the company is mine. Fifty-fifty.'

A doll with a ripcord.

'I own half.' *Sniff.* 'I know I do.'

Zee speaks, but the words he says do not compute.

'I own half,' repeats David, ignoring him.

Zee speaks again. Slowly.

'David,' he sighs. 'Your deal is no secret. You are to receive fifty per cent of the profits – after your expenses are deducted – of the monies generated by you and you alone. You own no portion of Mainman. Mainman belongs exclusively to Tony.'

'No.' *Sniff.* 'I own half.'

'No. You don't.'

'No! *You're* wrong.' *Sniff.* 'I . . . I . . . I own . . .'

'*Nothing.*' Zee wags his head. 'You own nothing. Don't you see? It's not your company, David. It's Tony's. His company. His money. You work for Tony. I work for Tony. Everyone works for Tony.'

Zee's words hang in the air like tear gas.

David inhales, splutters and suffocates.

Time chokes with him and the Earth ceases to spin. Till with numb fingers he shakes a cigarette to his lips, fumbles a lighter, trembles a flame and weakly puffs. Outside, the night sky softly reddens with the encroaching threat of day. The dawn of a hard new reality.

Aeons pass before David speaks again. But when he does it's not clear who he's talking to. An omnipotent god, Zee, Benjamin Franklin or the pathetic face staring up from the mirror. The dumbest of them all.

'Why? . . . Why did it come to . . . *this*?'

'MIRROR, MIRROR ON THE WALL, who's the fattest of them all?'

'Still you, Mama. Still you.'

Not as fat as she was. Dropping 5 stone down from her heaviest of 21, ignoring all medical advice by fasting on a crash diet that's already seen her hospitalised once this year. 'I won't be satisfied,' she says, 'until I can walk into a shop and buy a dress off the peg.' Though at 16 stone she's still a whopper. But then would anyone recognise Cass if she wasn't?

It's what the packed stalls of the Palladium have paid their £2.50 to see. The fat one from the Mamas & the Papas starring in her own cabaret, rising up from the stage in a diamante frock like the sugar plum fairy trilling 'Dream A Little Dream Of Me'. And London loves her for it. The last Saturday night of her two-week run and they pack her off with a standing ovation. Five thousand palms united in a semaphore of '*Nice-one-fatso!*'

Blinded by bouquets, she waddles back to her dressing room so elated she leaves a lipstick message on the mirror for next week's crowdpuller, Hollywood star Debbie Reynolds.

'*Dear Debbie, if they're half as nice to you as they were to me you will have a great time. Love, Cass.*'

As she scribbles good luck to a woman less than half her body weight she has no idea that Debbie and her 17-year-old daughter, Carrie, are already leaving the swinging Chelsea townhouse Cass herself is heading to as soon as she's out the stage door. Today, Mick Jagger turns 31 and while he'd never risk soiling his own Cheyne Walk carpet with canapés trodden under celebrity shoe leather he would that of an interior designer who lives round the corner. Arriving at the address in Tite Street, Cass is waved in past three muscular Stones security men, bounces over the threshold, turns a corner and with a flip in her stomach sees a crash diet crash landing. Salvers of smoked salmon, smoked trout, sliced chicken, cold pheasant, the whole interior salon wreathed floor to ceiling in melon, strawberries, blueberries, peaches and an oasis of fresh fruits: if she wanted, she could literally lick the walls.

The other guests mostly lick each other. The newly cropped birthday boy, who yesterday told *The Sun* he's just been in New York talking about making a possible film with David Bowie – because who isn't these days? – suited in buttercup yellow. His exotic wife in a blush-pink Zandra Rhodes creation and matching headdress, her make-up by Pierre Laroche, also here in leather. The ubiquitous Ossie Clark in blue. Bryan Ferry in grey. Britt Ekland in velvet. Rod Stewart incorrigible. And Angie, wife of David Bowie, here alone in a sexy satin cheongsam with matching black stilettos. Between the rock disco inside and the string quartet in the garden, all having the most 'FAAABULOUS' time.

So does Cass, trying hard not to eat anything and even harder not to think about throwing it up should she cave. Her home-from-home is a Mayfair flat loaned to her by Harry Nilsson where she crushes the mattress springs around dawn, stealing what little sleep she can before a Sunday brunch appointment in her honour over in Holland Park. Cass looks excusably tired, but not so much she doesn't stay almost five hours, washing down Chinese food, fruit salad and whipped cream with apple juice. Nor is she so tuckered by one shindig she doesn't roll straight onto another in Kensington where the American writer Jack Martin supplies her all the cheese, soda, David Hemmings and Alan Bates she can stomach. But after nearly twenty hours of non-stop revelling she's politely pecked, gingerly grazed and nervously nibbled all she can.

Sunday evening, the summer sky still a cloudless blue, Cass returns to the flat in Curzon Place, her body exhausted but her restless stomach rumbling for a glass of Coca-Cola and a ham sandwich. She places both on her bedside table, switches on the television, strips off her clothes and sprawls on top of the covers, head propped up on her pillows. Her eyes are heavy. So is her breathing. Shortly after 1.30 a.m., another house guest returns late and hears Cass snoring as they tiptoe past her room. The last sound anyone ever remembers her making.

Because on Monday afternoon, her secretary knocks, enters and finds the TV still on, the Coca-Cola barely sipped, the ham sandwich untouched and the naked body of 32-year-old Cass Elliot dead of a heart attack.

Long before the coroner concludes it was her obesity and the strain of her yo-yo starvation diets that killed her, the public have already gorged themselves sick on too many headlines quoting the first physician on the scene. His rash misdiagnosis that she fatally choked on a ham sandwich which never even reached her lips. And so the legend of poor old Mama Cass, the fattest of them all, writes itself. A tragic story with a profoundly miserable moral.

Some people just can't live with what they see staring back in the mirror.

FOURTEEN

HE TOLD THEM HE WAS COMING. Last month when he was here for five nights at the Tower. The same *Diamond Dogs* show, night after night, and they camped out till dawn to buy orchestra tickets for all five. Soon as he got here the name of his hotel beat out on the Philly jungle drums. *The–Belle–vue–Strat–ford–South–Broad–Street!* Every day they'd lie in ambush next door at the Harvey House diner, nursers of one coffee and a donut between them, waiting to pounce with pens and albums and Instamatic cameras. And when they did, quaking as they watched him fill the empty speech bubbles on their copies of *The Man Who Sold The World* with 'Love on ya, Bowie '74', he didn't just scribble and run. He stopped and spoke to them. He was interested. In *them*. Because they lived in Philadelphia, city of brotherly love and the Three Degrees. Children of David's promised land.

'I'm coming back,' he'd said, between sniffs. 'In about a month, once the tour's finished, I'm going to be doing some recording here. Sigma Sound studio. So, you know,' then with an enticing smile, 'keep an eye out for me.'

Sigma Sound. Easy to find as flicking through a phone book. An unassuming two-storey building way up skid row around 12th and Race, sandwiched between the winos of Saint John's Hospice and the hookers of Chinatown. About a month, he'd said, and that was five weeks ago, when Nixon was still president and Christine Chubbuck still had a pulse. Keep your eyes out, he'd told them, and soon as he said it theirs have barely shut. They take it in turns, cruising up and down past shoeless bums and signs for chop suey, sharing daily dispatches with one another by phone. No sign today. No sign tomorrow. Maybe try the Bellevue hotel again. No sign there either. No sign anywhere. Just the sidewalks of Center City with a Bowie-shaped hole in them.

And then one night, a different call. A few minutes after Marla drives past Sigma and sees a blue Cadillac that looks a lot like the blue Cadillac he used to dash in and out of outside the Bellevue. She double-checks the licence plate. Registered New York State.

Her scream all but shatters the payphone glass.

'HE'S HEEEERE!'

HE'S THERE. Inside. Waiting.

Waiting for a package to arrive, driven direct from a trusted supplier 100 miles away in Manhattan. When the package arrives, David can start. Until then, he can't. Until then, he waits.

When David waits, everyone must wait with him. Tony, his producer, who'll be sharing some of the package, otherwise he'll probably fall asleep. Almost everyone else here does fall asleep at some point or other unless they dip in the package. David typically arrives, and waits, halfway through the evening. The package usually turns up by midnight at the latest, and as soon as it does, work begins and doesn't stop until five, six, maybe seven in the morning. It's hard to last that long if you're not dipping in the package and nobody lasts longer and dips deeper than David. That's why Tony dips too, only some nights purely to keep his lids from slamming he dips a little too deep and a little too often, till his heart starts jackhammering so violently he has to chew a jar of sleeping pills to feel vaguely normal again. This is what happens when you try and keep up with David. Because nobody can.

The clock says ten. Still no package.

David counts down in cigarettes in a swivel chair behind the mixing console. His flightdeck to the Milky Way. All these months listening and dreaming and now he's finally sat in the cockpit. Dust those channel faders for prints and you'd still find the index fingers of Gamble and Huff. These, the same gain knobs twiddled for the Three Degrees. That, the level monitor needle that danced off its hinge for Harold Melvin's 'The Love I Lost'. There, through that glass, the very microphone where Billy Paul made a four-second meal of 'Me And' before he got to 'Mrs Jones'. And over in the corner, the none-more-holy MFSB hi-hat that snapped sweet syncopation into 'TSOP'. All created here, and maybe some of their magic dust still lying around for David to sweep up and sprinkle over his new album. Soon as the other magic dust gets here.

Ten fifteen. No package.

He has the flightdeck but not the cabin crew. He wanted to record at Sigma, he wanted the same MFSB house band and he wanted Gamble and Huff sat at the controls. He gets one out of three. When you're Black America's number 1 hit factory you don't need no English whitey rolling up asking to scratch his back for a few extra dollars. But at least they gave him two weeks in their studio.

That's why he's had to bring Tony back and put together his own band. Not quite MFSB, though he has the consolation of borrowing their conga player, Larry. From New York, he brings Ava as backing vocalist and the only two *Diamond Dogs* tour musicians to survive his cull, Garson on keys and another David, the saxophonist. He has a fresh funky rhythm section, Willie and Andy, between them the soul chops of Sly & The Family Stone, Donny Hathaway and Stevie Wonder. And, also from New York, a young Puerto Rican guitarist who's played with James Brown, appeared on *Sesame Street* and not lost an atom of cool in the switch between. As nerdy a bespectacled face as ever dared grow an afro, Carlos Alomar arrives at Sigma in triplicate, accompanied by his wife, Robin, and Luther, their best friend who buckles his belt round about the same notch as Barry White. They both sing, Carlos tells David, which he doesn't fully appreciate till he overhears them lounging on the control-room sofa, casually adlibbing harmonies to a rough playback. Two minutes later they're on the other side of the glass, stood around a mic with an English voice in their ears coaxing them to 'Do that *aawwwwl-right!* bit again'. And his nine-strong mostly black Sigma band is complete.

Ten thirty. No package.

Complete and scratching their chins, their scalps, the cracks of their arses, yawning and waiting while David waits. And smokes. And thinks.

And wonders. What it is he's doing. The new sound he's chasing and the new songs he's singing. A black soul sound and words about love and heartache, and come back baby, and boogying down with Davey. An album that he might simply call *Dancin'*, or perhaps *The Gouster*, or his current favourite, *Shilling The Rubes*. A record no listener would ever connect with the artist who sang 'Rock 'N' Roll Suicide' that may itself be a conscious act of commercial suicide. Which, maybe, wouldn't be so bad now David knows what he's become. Mainman's leading brand of soda pop.

BOWIE by Mainman! It's the real thing! Every time, that same ol' clear, crisp taste! Come alive, you're in the BOWIE by Mainman generation! Pure as sunlight! The only thing like BOWIE by Mainman is BOWIE by Mainman itself!

It's all Defries has ever cared about. Generating more licensed product to sell by the box, the pallet, the truck, the convoy, the warehouse. And there's nothing David can do to stop the selling. But he does have the power to sabotage the brand. Change the flavour. Crash the business. Piss off his foreman. Send Defries the funkiest 'fuck off!' he can. Shill the rube who's been shilling him.

Ten forty-five.

A buzz on the intercom pops David's thoughts like bubblegum. His head whips round to the woman picking up the receiver on the wall. He doesn't say it, but his eyes beg it.

The package?

Trying her efficient best to mask her dismay, Corinne looks back at David and nods.

THEY CATCH HIM OFF GUARD. When he's packaged to the eyeballs, a fedora shielding his eyes from the pinkening sky promising another humid August day, stepping out of Sigma straight into their human barricade. A swarm of saucer-eyed kids in their late teens, a few boys but mostly girls, some in the Bowie T-shirts they bought at his recent Tower shows, others with Ziggy cuts, shaved eyebrows, hennaed hair and flaking eyeshadow.

The unmistakable tribal markings of his devout Moonage Daydreamers. They follow him to the car, circling like gulls, squawking his name as Stuey delicately shoves him forward with a hand at the base of his spine. Then, because they've watched enough sodas turn flat at the Harvey House this week to know he's not in the Bellevue, one of them asks him. 'David, where are you staying?'

Before his speeding brain has time to process who they are, why they're here at this hour and whether he should lie or not, David sniffs sharply and tells them.

'The Barclay.'

Where the blue Cadillac driven by Jim the Lim speeds off not five seconds later.

THE PHILLY JUNGLE DRUMS beat hard and fast.

The–Bar–clay–on–the–south–east–cor–ner–of–Rit–ten–house–Square!

The next evening they're hawking the entrance long before Jim the Lim rolls up around six. Most of them have been here all afternoon. The kids from last night and others just like them, the ones who get called 'freaks' and 'faggots' at high school because they wear make-up and listen to *Aladdin Sane* instead of wearing plaid and listening to the Grateful Dead. Here with tiny cameras dangling on straps round their wrists and necks, more *Diamond Dogs* T-shirts and Ziggy cuts, gripping yet more marker pens, records, posters and magazines.

Through the gold-plated glass doors they first see his fedora bobbing through the lobby between the heads of Stuey and Corinne. He sees them soon as his brogues kiss sunlight. But a man who starts his working day waiting is never in any rush. So he stops, and he talks to them, and he signs their LPs, and he has his picture taken. And every signature, every look into the lens, every word that shyly slips from his lips feels like they're witnessing a miracle. Ink and camera film. Loaves and fishes.

Then he's in the car, slowly rolling northwards on the short one-mile journey to Sigma. In the backseat, he lights a cigarette and cracks open a can of beer, gliding up South 18th with the taste of sweet malt and nicotine. He's not itching, not yet, but he knows it's coming. The itch, the wait, the package, the scratch.

The Cadillac turns right onto Race, braking at a red light jumped by a silver-and-red Chevy Camaro screeching out from behind. David doesn't take much notice as he sips and puffs and twitches a knee to the tune blaring inside his head. The light turns green and the car breezes on. Two more blocks, then left into 12th where David sees them long before Jim slows to a rest behind a hastily parked silver-and-red Chevy Camaro. More kids. Only when he peers through the windscreen and sees their faces, he realises. They're the *same* kids. Burning rubber, jumping lights and risking pile-ups to get here before he did. Just so they can see him, again, going in. And still be here at god knows what hour, to see him, again, going out. The waiting game outside, same as the waiting game in.

Tonight, once the package arrives, after multiple takes and infinite dips, at around 4 a.m. David calls time to listen to a playback. When the tape finishes he asks Tony, 'Can we hear that last one again?' Then to no one in particular, 'Are they still there?'

Corinne volunteers to poke her head downstairs where their silhouettes merge into a giant blob behind the reception glass. 'Still there,' she reports back. David checks the clock, juts his chin, jerks an eyebrow and balances another cigarette on his bottom lip. Then sinks back and smokes it with a cagey crooked smile.

STILL THERE. That morning when he leaves and the following afternoon waiting outside the Barclay. Jumping the same reds to race him to the studio and tomorrow night, all through the night, till he leaves again, on the sidewalk, huddled by the door, sneaking into bars a few blocks into Chinatown whenever they need to use the john. Still there, because they're *always* there, never being any trouble. And being no trouble, and being just kids, they're not just tolerated. They're adopted, like stray cats to be fed and cared for.

Their charm quickly rubs off on a studio engineer who obligingly wedges open the second-floor window of the control room in the hope they get to hear some music in the alleyway below. They win the affection of Stuey, who they take record shopping, and Carlos and his wife Robin, who invite a lucky few to their hotel room to listen to each day's tape of

David's work in progress. Every day Jim the Lim stands back and allows them to invade the backseat of the Cadillac like a tribe of monkeys as they scavenge for souvenirs: stray strands of orange Bowie hair, the empty can he drank from, crumpled tissues and cigarette butts – *so* many cigarette butts. They're sometimes brought coffee and sandwiches, and if ever the studio sends out for hot food, the kids are always asked if they'd like anything. And every night Corinne or some other messenger appears at the door to check whether any of them need a few dollars for the cab fare to ensure they get home safe. David insists. Now that they've joined the few people in his life he can rely on.

This much he knows. Sure as the sickness in his gut when he shuts his eyes and casts his mind back two summers. A June night in 1972. Flying in from London, straight into a limo from JFK to watch Elvis at the Garden with Angie, Ronno and Defries.

The three heroes in his life. His scarecrow, tinman and lion. Off to see the wizard.

And one by one, starting with Ronno, they all let him down.

Angie. How can he rely on her anymore? After this week when she flew in, discovered Ava is with him, turned into Norma Desmond, threatened to kill herself, trashed David's hotel room, then flew out again. And Defries? He's long past relying on that prickly deceiver, no less apoplectic in his own icier Defriesian manner when he visited the studio to check productivity and near swallowed his stogie when he heard what's happened to his brand BOWIE. All that unnecessary drama when those two ought to know better than anyone else they can chuck all the bitter words and bedside lamps they like. David doesn't do confrontation.

No. Old alliances are dead and battle lines drawn. All he has left is Corinne, and Stuey, and Tony, and whichever musicians and paramours he rotates to do his bidding. And these kids outside with their unconditional love. His Sigma disciples. His Philly babies. These kids, he can depend on. These kids, David needs.

Almost as much as the package.

THERE ARE JUST TEN OF THEM.
Patti, Marla, Leslie, Lenni, Barbara, Linda, Pat, Jimmy, Joey and Ernie.

The ones there every night, no matter how hot or cold or wet or hungry or late. The ones with fast cars and a seeming death wish who race him every day from the hotel to the studio and back again. The ones who never get bored, who never give in and leave early, who wouldn't budge from the steps of Sigma if a category five tornado tore down 12th Street. And the only ones who happen to be there the yawning dawn David appears like a messianic vision with a holy commandment. 'We're finishing in a few days,' he begins. 'So I'd really like to invite you up to listen to what we've done. Be here the night after tomorrow, but *just* you people who are here right now. Don't tell anyone else.' Then, with a wink, he raises and drops the rim of his fedora. 'Keep it under your hat.'

The vow of silence is easy. Less so the getting rid of the other uninvited Bowie kids who purely by chance show up two nights later to join their stakeout. It doesn't help that Patti and Marla and their gang are dressed in their best going-out clothes. And suspiciously fidgety. And unusually pessimistic about any chance of seeing David this side of daybreak.

'Oh no, we've heard he won't be out for *hours!*'

'Yeah, not till morning. Sucks, I know!'

'Aw, really, there's no point hanging around. Uh-huh, sure, try again tomorrow.'

The last straggler discouraged and sent sulking to their home, the tension eases. The coast now clear, it's just the chosen ones. They check their watches. Witching o'clock. Up above the darkness rumbles with the threat of rain. The faint echo of raised voices and breaking glass. The nearby wail of a police siren. Then a familiar click.

The front door opens. Corinne, her portcullis eyes calculating a head count. Ten of them. All present and correct.

'OK,' she says with the narrowest of smiles. 'You can come on up.'

HE'S EDGY AS A GETAWAY DRIVER, blazing through cigarette after cigarette, pacing up and down behind Tony in the control room, a loose pale blue suit, fat-knotted tie and oversized tinted glasses that make him look as goofy as Jerry Lewis's Nutty Professor. He catches his uneasy reflection as he watches the kids file into the main studio, ushered to the wonky ring of folding chairs where Carlos and the other musicians are waiting to greet them. They see him through the glass straight away and straight away wonder why he looks so nervous. He asks himself the same question. They're as dedicated as any fans ever to waggle a pen under his nose, but that's partly the fear. Look at them – best clothes, washed hair, new lipstick and freshly ironed T-shirts bearing his name. He knows they eat *Ziggy*, breathe *Diamond Dogs* and sleep *Space Oddity*. Just because they say they love *him* doesn't make them any less the number 1 consumers of Mainman brand BOWIE. And tonight they're about to have their faith tested as never before. What if they *hate* it? What if Defries is right? What if . . . ?

Only one way to find out. David leans over the mixing desk and presses the talkback button.

''Ullo,' he says Dick-Van-Dykely. They stare at him behind the glass like he's being beamed upon a giant TV screen. 'So what I'm gonna play you isn't finished. These are all rough tracks. But they're not like anything I've done in the past. It's very different.' He sniffs. 'So I wanted you to come and 'ave a listen and, uh, I'm very interested in what you all think.' *Sniff.* 'Thank you.'

Leaving Tony with the tape, David walks through the adjoining door, out of the TV into touchable reality, striding to the very back of the room near the piano. He sits down behind a curly-haired kid in a clownprint jacket. A nod to Tony. A second's silence. Then music.

Loud music. So loud their metal chairs become lightning rods, every bar conducted through their bones, thumping in their joints, throbbing up their spines, tingling their skulls. And funky. So funky that for the first few seconds even they forget it's David Bowie. Until they hear his voice. Then he sings his name. Then, at the chorus, they realise it's a new version of a song they already know, 'John, I'm Only Dancing'. Except the original was a bit like Carl Perkins. This one's more like Funkadelic.

None of it sounds like the Bowie they know. The guitars are slick and rhythmic, not the hard crunch of the Spiders or *Diamond Dogs*. The piano boogies and jellyrolls to a groovy offbeat. The arrangements are smothered in female harmonies, a lot like Labelle. There's a *hell* of a lot of saxophone, jazzing and Staxing between any crevice it can. Some of it shuffles, some has a light Latino swing, but much of it smooches to the babymaking beat of Barry White. And never before has David's singing been loaded with such raw emotion. He's the love-'em-'n'-leave-'em shitheel with a conscience of the closing-time ballad 'It's Gonna Be Me'. The promiscuous romantic of 'Can You Hear Me'. The grunting loverman of 'Right'. The browmopping bragger of 'Somebody Up There Likes Me'. The existential preacher of 'Who Can I Be Now?' The cheated dreamer of 'Young Americans'.

And the anxious star at the back of the room, rocking on his haunches, having smoked the best part of a plantation between the first track 45 minutes ago and the last just beginning to fade. The moment of truth now upon him. David suddenly jolts.

'PLAY IT AGAIN!'

The whole room jolts with him. The scream of a dark-haired girl in a roseprint dress named Lenni. Screamed at the pitch you normally hear 'FIRE!' A scream that makes the band laugh and David straighten up, mouth contorted in the slow ignition of an incredulous smile. *Really?*

'Yeah, play it again!'

'Please!'

'I love it!'

David's eyes bounce from face to face. Patti, shimmering in her golden skirt with her *Diamond Dogs* dog-tag necklace. Jimmy in the same necklace with a white Bowie T-shirt. Joey in a black one with silver Ziggy boots. Can it be true? His ten disciples, and not one of them Judas?

'Alright, then,' he nods, smile reaching full speed. 'Tony? Let's hear it again.'

The second play, a party erupts. The kids up on their feet, dancing, drinking, smoking, laughing, jiving with David and his band to the sort of music they'd never jive to in their bedrooms papered floor to ceiling with his face. But then he's their immaculate exception. Even if tomorrow they'll have already forgotten half of what they hear, none will forget tonight as long as they live.

Nor will David. Because no package can ever disintegrate its memory. Not of this, the night his street urchins set him free. The ones who've shown him something his scarecrow, tinman and lion of old never could. Beyond the rainbow, deep in his soul.

Love on ya, Sigma kids! Love on ya, Philly!

There's no place like home.

★

THE SOUND OF HOME *is* the sound of Philadelphia. The two weeks David records there are the two weeks the Three Degrees top the UK chart with 'When Will I See You Again?' The second week, they're joined at number 2 by another Sigma crown jewel, The Stylistics' 'You Make Me Feel Brand New'. The discotheques are changing. The beats are changing. Not just the dreamy Philly Sound but the electric boogaloo of George McCrae's 'Rock Your Baby' and the funky hotstep of Hues Corporation's 'Rock The Boat'. Because the beats are changing, the moves are changing, and because the moves are changing, the clothes are changing. The bottoms baggier, the cuts looser. Clothes to sweat in. Clothes to boogie in. Clothes to get down in.

Clothes you might find in Jac's in Barnstaple. 'The Younger Man's Shop' say its polka dot carrier bags, and here's a younger man walking out the door with one now. Inside, a fawn-coloured jumper by Pierre Sangan. Perfect for spinning on the dancefloor in a pair of Oxford bags to 'Queen Of Clubs' by KC & The Sunshine Band.

Except this younger man has other ideas. Half eleven at night on a bank holiday weekend he's creeping along the corridors of the Royal & Fortescue Hotel. He finds what he's looking for on the third floor in Room 39.

A seven-year-old girl, alone, in her bed.

He startles her.

'Don't worry,' he says, making a shush sign with a finger to his lips. 'Mummy's downstairs.'

Then presses a knife against her throat and starts to do what he came for.

Suddenly, a shriek behind him. He freezes. Mummy's upstairs.

He springs off the bed and runs for the door, shoving Mummy aside. Then Daddy appears. Daddy lands a punch on the younger man's head. A frantic scuffle, kicking and punching, Daddy desperate to hang on to him, clawing at his new jumper, the sleeves stretching like chewing gum when, like an eel, the younger man slips out of it, pelting in his undershirt out along the corridor, down the hotel stairs, into the night.

The North Devon constabulary are quick to react. Within a few hours they've sixty officers blocking every transport artery out of town. Thanks to Mummy and Daddy they've a very detailed description.

'The attacker is between 25 and 30, between 5 foot 8 and 5 foot 11, with a sallow complexion, high cheekbones and a cut on his left eye where the girl's father struck him. Light blond hair, short on top. The hairstyle is described as like David Bowie.'

Rule Bowietannia. Yet to forget him.

FIFTEEN

EMERGENCY MEETING OF THE BOARD OF DIRECTORS OF MAINMAN LTD

LOCATION: The frontal lobe of Tony Defries
TIME: Recurring, daily, nightly, late August 1974
DIRECTORS PRESENT: Tony Defries
CHAIR: Tony Defries
MINUTES TAKEN BY: The insomnia of Tony Defries
PURPOSE OF MEETING: Resolve urgent crisis in brand BOWIE

AGENDA

ITEM #1: Toxicity of Product

After thanking the board for their attendance at such short notice, Mr
Defries expressed regret that he had been placed in a position where he
was now forced to report the levels of toxins polluting the Product – as
has been monitored over the course of previous meetings – has become
unacceptable. According to Mr Defries, the Product has surrendered all
discretion on the issue so as to become, in his words, 'wilfully defiant' to
any discussion of its detriment to long-term company yield. Mr Defries
then drew attention to the forthcoming arrival of Mr Yentob of the
BBC and his film crew who have been assigned to make an hour-long
commercial for brand BOWIE for future broadcast on British television.
The board shared Mr Defries's concern that any access to the Product by

Mr Yentob and his cameramen must be severely limited and at all times heavily chaperoned to insure against any instances of product toxicity finding its way into the finished television advertisement.
SOLUTION: Ongoing. Mr Defries informed the board that he has already issued verbal ultimatums and is still investigating those persons suspected of facilitation and supply in a concentrated effort to insulate the Product against any further deterioration in brand performance.

ITEM #2: Insubordination of Product

On a separate, though possibly not unconnected point, Mr Defries was equally sorry to inform the board of the Product's increasing noncompliance with company strategy apropos projected targets and market growth. The board were alarmed to hear the Product had taken it upon themselves to ignore the sales patterns of consecutive previous periods and 'rebrand' brand BOWIE without prior consultation. Mr Defries stated that the Product's recent output, the first to be manufactured at a new plant in Philadelphia, fell so far short of consumer expectancy as to be substandard. Also at risk is the company investment in the staging of the Product's registered *Diamond Dogs* tour, the costs yet to be recouped. It is the Product's stubborn proposal that the resumption of said North American tour as scheduled this autumn should proceed without said costly production assets, effectively writing off a loss. As Mr Defries surmised, this amounted to a shocking disregard for any financial impact to the company and would almost certainly 'torpedo' all fiscal objectives for the final quarter.
SOLUTION: Mr Defries assured the board that on the issue of brand identity, he was confident the market would be tested, and respond favourably, to the Product's imminent concert album *David Live* and its single, 'Knock On Wood', both amounting to a more subtle variation of consumers' expectations of the company trademark. The shipment date of the rogue Philadelphia stock itself has yet to be decided, pending further productivity and quality control checks. On the separate issue of the tour, Mr Defries was happy to report a compromise had been reached. The staging would be retained for the opening week of shows in Los Angeles, also to be filmed by Mr Yentob and his television crew, and four subsequent dates in California and Arizona. Thereafter the Product has been granted licence to revise the tour as they decide, under strictest cautions pertaining to the above.

Item #3: Future of Product

The aggregate of the aforementioned company liabilities being what they are, Mr Defries wished to reassure the board that, though the current situation could unequivocally be termed 'a crisis' and appropriate actions required to be taken to stabilise the Product's performance with the greatest of urgency, they ought not entertain any suggestion the global expansion of brand BOWIE is in jeopardy. Mr Defries reiterated that the terms of the manufacturing contract, as had been signed by the Product in their most recent binding agreement dated, at Mr Defries's own instruction, '31st September 1972', were such that ultimately the Product had 'no choice' but to subjugate to the will of the board and fulfil all legal duties according to production and delivery of materials and their mandatory promotion wherever the market requires. Mr Defries added that any prospect of industrial action on the part of the Product was extremely unlikely, precisely because of the non-negotiable provisos of their employment heretofore outlined.

Solution: Board satisfied.

Item #4: Any Other Competent Business

Mr Defries very briefly updated the board on his latest activities:

(1) Company capital apportioned to new Mainman theatre venture making excellent progress. Play *Fame* by Mr Ingrassia set for Broadway opening in November. Certain box office hit.

(2) Brand Mick Ronson still performing poorly. Shopfloor rumours of takeover bid/merger with Mott The Hoople unconfirmed.

(3) Investment in brand Dana Gillespie continuing despite dismal commercial reaction. Blame apportioned to possible undersell of obvious brand assets. Motion for new publicity materials with intensified focus on said assets granted.

(4) Bigger assets on horizon if successful addition to company portfolio of Raquel Welch. Board extremely excited. Negotiations developing.

(5) Mr Defries took a final vote on whether more profits from brand BOWIE be converted into gold bullion. Current price of $158 an ounce. Approval unanimous.

Solution: Meeting adjourned.

★

THERE IS NO FLY. There is a limousine rolling through the desert, there is David in the backseat, thin as a standard lamp with his fedora the shade, there is Corinne lounging opposite in a camisole dress, and there is the exhaustingly solemn Mr Yentob from the BBC, his cameraman and his sound recordist. But there is no fly.

There is, however, an elephant. In the room, in the car, in the backseat, under the hat.

Mr Yentob sees it but tries his professionally polite public schoolboy best to pretend it isn't there, just as he's been pretending since he landed in Los Angeles last week, his furrowed forehead shining with all sorts of bright ideas about the sort of documentary he hoped to make. The brightest borrowing its wattage from something David said in a TV interview with Russell Harty last year.

'I'm a collector. I've always just seemed to collect personalities.'

A trait Mr Yentob sought to expand upon as the dominant theme of a televisual thesis he plans on calling, perhaps predictably, *The Collector*. The only problem being that Mr Yentob's expectations are based on the forgivable assumption that the David he would be interviewing in September 1974 would be more or less the same David he saw being interviewed by Mr Harty in January 1973. Until he meets him. And, simultaneously, the elephant.

Mr Harty never met the elephant because when he interviewed David it wasn't there. But now that it is, dealing with David means dealing with the elephant. Except you can't. Like Angie says, trying to have a relationship with the elephant is like trying to eat an aircraft carrier. And Mr Yentob has been chewing on runway all week.

The elephant has made filming not merely difficult but often impossible. Despite all Defries's promises of unprecedented access prior to his arrival, so far Mr Yentob's on-camera time with David has been pathetically brief. The elephant would rather David didn't come out to play, and on the sporadic stolen moments he does, it's the elephant who speaks. Like right now. That's not David sitting in the backseat, gurning '*ah-oo!*' to a tape of Aretha Franklin. It's the elephant. An elephant that lives on cigarettes and low-fat milk and bag after bag of elephant powder. An elephant that doesn't trumpet, only sniffs, and every time David sniffs, there's the elephant.

Sniff.

Corinne hears it too, but being with the elephant every day Corinne is as good as deaf and blind to it. She knows what it is and where it is, just as she knows she can't do anything to stop it. If she could, she'd shoot the elephant and mount its head on the wall above her bed as a permanent trophy of her undying love for David. But the only one who can shoot the elephant is David himself. And so without ever loving it, she lives with it, for his sake covering its tracks when necessary with her damage-limiting efficiency, patiently praying for the day when he wakes up and pulls the trigger.

'*Ah-oo!*'

But why would David want to when they're having this much fun together? Ah-ooing along to Aretha in the back of a nice shiny big car, dipping their trunks in a lovely carton of sweet, sweet milk. *Shoot it?* Gawd, no! That'd be silly. Not when the elephant is the only one who truly loves him. The only one who *gets* him. The only one who'll listen to him when he wants to chatter for hours and hours about the charisma of Adolf Hitler, or the enigma of Howard Hughes, or how the ancient Mayans established contact with outer space. Not when the elephant protects him. From *them.* Stops him seeing what they all see. Because they see David and they see frail, they see starved, they see sallow, they see mad, they see cancer wards, Belsen and the Biafran famine, they see Murnau's *Nosferatu* and Munch's *The Scream*, they see Brian Jones, Jim Morrison, Janis and Jimi, all dead at his age of 27, and a plot in the same cemetery with David's name on it.

Which is why he needs the elephant. Like a safety blindfold, keeping him in the darkness.

'*Ah-oo!*'

Ach, you've got to laugh. And they do, David and the elephant. Have a right laugh. They've got to when everyone else is so bloody serious all the time. Like him over there with his camera whatsit. Always poking it in their faces. Who is he again? Mr Ying Tong Iddle I Po or something? What's he yapping on about now?

'Since you've been in America, you seem to have picked up on a lot of the idioms and themes in American music, American culture. How's that happened?'

Right, come on, elephant. Let's give him a cracker.

'There's a . . .'

Hee-hee!

'. . . There's a fly floating around in my milk and he's a foreign body in it, you see, and . . .'

Haw-haw!

'. . . he's getting a lot of milk . . .'

HA-HA!

'. . . It's kind of how I feel.'

Heh! Nice one, elephant. Because there is no fly.

SHE DOESN'T SEE HIS ELEPHANT but then she's blinded by her own. A treacly-coloured one from Tennessee swishing in her handbag, name of Jack. Jack makes her every waking moment sparklier than all those fat rocks around her neck, in her ears and on her fingers. Diamonds are meant to be a girl's best friend, but she knows Jack's an even better one. He's the only man never to let her down, not like the other hopheads, dopeheads, gamblers and cheats. Soon as she marries Jekyll she's on a honeymoon with Hyde. Five down and she still never learns, but nor do they. On bended knees telling her she's the most beautiful woman in the world, showering her with jewels, giant pearls, mink coats, fur-upholstered Rolls-Royces, villas, yachts and private jets. Then soon as she's out of sight they fuck the first pancake waitress with bigger jugs than the maple syrup.

Burton. *Bastard.*

They were married ten years. The divorce hearing took 15 minutes. She never dreamed she could live without Burton but so long as she has bourbon she doesn't have to. Dream, that is. Just carry on existing as a stinking rich, suffocatingly famous, newly single 42-year-old screen goddess. Not that the speculating headlines ever stop.

'*Who is going to be the sixth Mr Liz Taylor?*'

Bookies' favourite is 39-year-old Dutchman Henry Wynberg, a used car salesman from Beverly Hills. Liz has just set up home with him in a gaudy mansion in Bel Air with metallic wallpaper in the master boudoir which acts as a pornographic hall of mirrors when they're in bed together. She's also demanding that he be given a crew job on her next film, a remake of the children's fantasy *The Blue Bird*, due to shoot in Russia. Even before her decree absolute, Henry's has been the very public arm around her kaftan. She likes it when the flashbulbs pop, likes to think how big they'll run the picture, likes to think of Burton flicking through the paper and stopping when he sees her smiling arm in arm with Henry, likes to think he'll see the glowing face of a woman sexually satisfied by a man ten years his junior, likes to think of him tearing the page to confetti, purple veins popping out of his forehead, roaring obscenities in Welsh so loud he'll level the Rhondda Valley to a gravel pit. Likes it almost as much as she likes Jack.

They're both with her tonight. Jack in her bag, Henry on her arm. All three watching David on the stage of the Anaheim Convention Center, glittering in the spotlight, bright as any kiss-and-make-up stone Burton ever bought her.

Liz likes what she sees. So does Jack, and since Jack has the final word what Henry thinks isn't of any importance. He sure can't stop her requesting a private audience once the show is over. And because she is who she is, because wherever she goes she's still the Queen of the Nile, kindred of Horus and Ra, daughter of Isis, beloved of the moon and sun, she receives it. In Governor Reagan's California as in Caesar's Rome, nobody keeps Cleopatra waiting. Not even Corinne with her sturdiest clipboard.

She jounces into the dressing room like a 12-stone 'Ta-dah!' David's ears supply their own fanfare. He is an instant flap of flattered charm. She, an uncoiling outrage of regal seduction, batting lashes large as one of her Egyptian slaves' ostrich feather fans. A couple of sweeps and a sketch forms. She sees he is a lot younger and a lot slimmer than Henry, with a cheeky English accent, eyes out of Tiffany's window, great hair, terrific cheekbones, thin but juicy lips and baggy trousers exciting suspicion their design has less to do with style than a priority for airflow around large artefacts within. He is masculine without being macho, sexy with an almost feminine elegance. She's known his type before. Delicate. When she speaks, he blushes. When he speaks, she giggles. She doesn't see the elephant. He never notices Jack. On first blurred impressions, a perfect match.

Who she's thinking of when she makes love with her Dutchman later that night Jack doesn't ask. Just waits till it's over when Henry rolls off and falls asleep so he and Liz can continue their conversation until the hour comes to jump her own Z-train.

So where were they?

This young man David. He liked her, didn't he? Naturally, says Jack. So he's staying at the Beverly Wilshire all month while he's rehearsing in LA. Should she ask him over to dinner? Obviously, says Jack. And didn't David mention he wanted to get into movies? Maybe she should cast him as her co-star in *The Blue Bird*? Absolutely, agrees Jack. And what if they courted advance publicity for the film and had their picture taken together for one of the celebrity magazines. Imagine Burton's rage! To see his precious Helen of Troy embracing a poncey young Englishman 20 years younger than him. *Englishman!* Oh, she *must*, insists Jack. Wear David around town as if he were one of her priceless jewels. Take him to parties. Add him to the other beautiful human trinkets she surrounds herself with, just as she's always done.

Yes, Jack, Liz drools sleepily. *Yes, like you say, just as I've always done. Same as I did with Jimmy, and Rock, and poor Monty. And now David . . . You see, I'm a collector, aren't I, Jack? Yes . . . I've always just seemed to collect personalities . . .*

HE DOESN'T HAVE AN ELEPHANT. He has a whole herd. Enough for a circus. You wouldn't want to see what's been shitting in his head and even he's scared to look. But then he doesn't have to. He knows what's been up there. Dope, smack, acid, coke, brandy, whisky, vodka, every animal in the whole fucking zoo. All that trampling it's amazing he's even got any brain left, and what he has you could scoop out and dish up like a Neapolitan ice cream. A strawberry strip of sarcasm, chocolate anger and a vanilla slab of hurt. But mix them together any way you like, it's the same cold sweet madness.

Of course *he* doesn't think he's mad. So he goes out one night pissed as an owl with a sanitary towel stuck on his forehead and some waitress calls him 'an asshole'. He just thinks he's being funny. Then that's Hollywood for you. It's why he packed it in and moved back to New York, where life is *real*. And he should know, now that he's living in a penthouse a couple of doors down from Greta Garbo where he likes to stand naked on the roof terrace watching flying saucers. Mad, me arse!

Still, here he is, back in the parking lot they call Los Angeles, waiting for Cleopatra. It's the only reason he came out tonight because Elton told him Cleo'll be there, otherwise he'd be back down the Troubadour slapping more sanitary towels on his head. Forty minutes he's been here, up in some mansion in the hills, but no sign of her highness yet. Just cocktails and canapés, and whatsisname junior, and daughter of thingummybob, and ex-wife of so-and-so, and the usual chickadees in lime green eyesores by Emilio Pucci comparing carats and skin cancers, all of them gawping at him over the rim of their martinis.

When in she blasts. Like a gas explosion destroying every other personality in the room. It almost cracks his specs. I mean, yeah, he's *famous*. He still gets recognised everywhere he goes. 'It's me nose,' he says. Sometimes cabbies come right out and ask. 'Are you . . . ?' And he answers before they finish. 'No, but I wish I 'ad his money.' But Cleo, it's not enough to call her a *star*. Look at her. That's a *comet*.

Streaking towards him in a pink paisley fireball of knockers and jewellery with those eyes crackling like the Kama Sutra and that smile of hers that could eat a man whole and spit out his balls like orange pips.

And now in his face, saying his name, instantly silencing his inner smartarse who thinks twice about greeting her as 'Dizzy Miss Lizzie'. On one side of him, Elton has already disintegrated. On the other, the Oriental woman everybody assumes to be named Yoko, but isn't, vanishes into thin air. It is just the pair of them, alone, in Caesar's tent, a full moon over the Nile. Lights! Camera! Action!

OK, Cleo, you be you, girl, and I'll be Rex Harrison in a toga. And . . . ah fook, who's this? Mark bloody Anthony?

From the corner of his eye another figure approaches, thin as a skewer and red on top, a human safety match draped in a mustard suit.

Is that . . . ?

Well, well, well! *Him!* Only the other day he was talking about *him*. When he had old Ray from the *Maker* up in his apartment, his two kittens Major and Minor running round their feet, eating a Chinese takeaway and watching cable when that band came on. He thought they were OK, even if they sounded terrible, and he liked their name. 'Television'. But it was their clothes that got him, just four scruffs in street rags.

'Hey, they've outdone Bowie!' he'd said to Ray. 'Bowie went crazy, and they've gone the other way.'

And now, here he is, the man himself. Crazy Davey Bowie. Maybe not dressed quite as crazy as he thought. And he seems to know Elton. And – *Christ!* – he must already know Cleo? Because now she's introducing them.

'David,' she says, 'do you know John?'

Does he know him? Oh, Cleo, don't do it to the poor bastard. Because the same thing always happens when any of *them* meet *him*. They stand there, bad actors at Mr Cool when if they shat themselves any harder it'd be sluicing down their ankles. Once bigger than Jesus, always bigger than Jesus.

Not easy being a legend, is it, Cleo? But then we always try our best to make them feel as OK we can, don't we, girl?

'Hi,' he says, shaking David's hand. 'I'm Johnny Beatle.'

THIS IS WHAT IT IS to be David Bowie now. It never used to be, not even six months ago. Back then he was still the kind of person who'd sidle into Malcolm's shop on the King's Road asking to make a T-shirt from a photo of Liz Taylor kneeling at the feet of James Dean in a mock crucifixion pose. Now he's the kind of person who has Liz Taylor in his dressing room, who gets invited round her house only to accidentally lock himself in her bathroom, who she sends scripts hoping he'll agree to co-star with her in her next film, who she rings up in his hotel suite flirting soft and breathily into the receiver asking if she can come and watch him in rehearsal with his band. The flat image upon the cinema screen is now round flesh in his arms. He knows what she smells and tastes like: Bal à Versailles and whiskey with an e. That same woman in that photo with Jimmy Dean, who starred with him in *Giant*, has looked David in the eye and told him that he, David, reminds her, Liz, of Jimmy. This is now his normal.

It's the same with John. Once upon a time he was just a magic voice coming out of David's record player. Then he wrote about him in 'Life On Mars?' Then he started singing one of his songs, 'This Boy'. Then a few weeks ago he was in a studio in Philadelphia stealing a line from his

'A Day In The Life' for his own 'Young Americans'. And now, thanks to Liz, they've met, and exchanged numbers, and made plans to catch up again once David's back in New York. These are just the sort of everyday things that now happen to him. The kind of people he collects. Cleopatra and the Eggman.

Because he's finally crossed over to the other side. This may be his normality, but it's not reality. David doesn't live there anymore. He's walked up out of the stalls and stepped into the screen. He lives inside the movie now, where everything and everyone is in Technicolor, his days directed by Walt Disney, his nights by Vincente Minnelli, the reels always changing, the end credits never in sight. The show always going on and on and on. And if he wasn't him, if he was anyone weaker, the psychedelic shock of it all probably *would* send him right off his rocker. But not David. Nah.

He takes it all with a pinch of his favourite salt.

SIXTEEN

MR MURPHY CANNOT DECIDE. If he could, they wouldn't be queuing out the door of the ABC on Reading's Friar Street not long gone ten o'clock on a Saturday morning. Not quite the 'stampede' feared by the cinema boss, but no danger of any of the 600 seats remaining empty. Around 150 of them have been reserved for an invited select committee of teachers, parents, clergymen, social workers and probation officers. The rest, there to be claimed on a first-come-first-served basis to any adult fulfilling the advertised open call –

> ## FREE FILM
> **Have you children aged 14 to 18 years or are you involved in the welfare of this group in any way? If so you are invited to a private screening of a new feature film . . .**

On the way to their seats they pass the poster for this week's main draw, Hammer's new kung fu horror *The Legend of the 7 Golden Vampires*, an X certificate. But that isn't this morning's chosen feature, its title still a secret. As is its certificate. Because Mr Murphy of the British Board of Film Censors cannot decide.

Because he can't, Reading must decide for him. For the first time ever, a UK film certificate is to be determined by the reaction of a public screening. All the test audience know in advance is that it definitely contains 'bad language and two sex scenes' which is why, at the end, they'll be asked to answer a questionnaire on its suitability for young audiences. The crux being whether Mr Murphy concedes to the wishes of its producers and awards it an AA for ages 14 and over, or an X, stigmatising it among the ID-challenging forbidden fruit of *The Exorcist*, that steamy new *Emmanuelle* and those seven karate-kicking bloodsuckers outside. The only other clue as to what they're about to watch being a not-too-subtle hint in the local *Evening Post*.

'*The film dealing with the rise and fall of a pop star is a sequel to a highly successful 1973 production.*'

So it falls upon the moral sensibilities of some random berks in Berkshire to decide the fate of *Stardust*.

Mr Murphy is here this morning, as is the film's producer, Mr Puttnam, sat at the back of the cinema, crossing his legs and savouring the buffet of his left-hand fingernails as the lights begin to fade. In front of him, the silhouettes of several hundred strangers' heads who have it in their power to financially ruin a film he's been sweating over for the last year, its revenue entirely dependent on reaching its intended teenage audience. With any luck, it should be on general release next month, just as its star, David Essex, is bringing out a new single and album and going on his first major UK tour. The best free publicity the film could have – unless the kids who buy his records and tickets aren't allowed to see it. Which is for this morning's jury to determine. On trial, two hours of sex, drugs, rock, roll and a man in a wig singing a choral Mass in an aircraft hangar. All Mr Puttnam can do is pray.

The two hours passed, when the lights rise again God sends him a messenger. A sinewy man in a dog collar with a face as sad as an empty collection plate. Mr Puttnam braces himself for the trembling finger of damnation.

'I don't like pop music,' the vicar says bluntly. 'But it's a good film.'
Heaven has spoken.

Reading concurs. The parents agree they'd bring their own kids to see it. The teachers praise its moral message. The social workers commend its honest treatment of ugly subjects. Why hide it from the kids, they say, when they, the fans, deserve to know the truth behind the glitter and the glamour? That the pop business is a cutthroat cesspit of treacherous egos, loveless sex, devious managers, financial chicanery, mental breakdowns and fatal addictions. That what happened to Brian and Jim and Janis and Jimi could still happen to anyone. Because they're still out there now, the Jim MacLaines of 1974. The face on the poster on a million bedroom walls, on a stage deafened by screams, in private jets and limousines, hiding in bathrooms from people they've made rich, off their cakes, waiting for the next package, counting down the seconds till they die of the overdose everyone around them who they pay not to say it sees coming.

But now the public have spoken, Mr Murphy decides.

'AA.' Alright for adolescents. The *Stardust* show *will* go on.

SEVENTEEN

THAT'S THE THING ABOUT THE SHOW. It always goes on. Even when it shouldn't.

Like that crazy bastard Bob from Montana. Every show he does nearly kills him. He's driven his hip bone through his pelvis. He's broken his lower spine. He's almost lost an arm with a compound fracture. But because he's not dead yet the show he calls Evel Knievel goes on. Even if it means trying to fire himself across a river canyon in Idaho – half a kilometre wide and twice the height of the Statue of Liberty – in a giant bullet. Powered by steam. Bob calls it his 'Skycycle' because it makes it sound like something Superman might fly, which is why he'll be sat in it in his usual flashy red, white and blue comic book hero costume. But it doesn't change the fact he's essentially a man jumping off a cliff strapped to a kettle.

Nobody believes he'll make it. Not the promoters and sponsors who are putting up around $6 million in what may as well be a life insurance payout. Not the 30,000 bloodthirsty clifftop spectators who pay $25 each hoping they'll see a deranged daredevil commit public suicide. Not his cousin, a Jesuit priest, who holds a service beside the launch ramp begging God to spare him. Not Bob's wife ironing her widow's weeds. Not even Bob himself. 'I have five backup systems,' says Bob. 'The fifth is called the Lord's Prayer.'

And every cotton-pickin' sonofabitch o' them is right.

Bob doesn't make it. Just blacks out upon launch, prematurely ignites the landing parachute and nosedives with a plop into the river below where the rescue boats drag him to safety with nothing worse than a bleeding nose.

The *Los Angeles Times* sums it up in one word: 'ABYSMAL'.

The swindled bikers watching above yell 'Hoax!' and start rampaging through the concession stands, looting beer and burning toilets.

Even the event promoter despairs. 'I don't care if I *ever* see Evel Knievel again!'

But for being stupid enough to try, useless enough to fail and lucky enough to live, Bob still gets to keep his estimated $6 million.

That's the thing about the show. It always goes on. Even when it shouldn't.

TWENTY-NINE DATES. Sixteen cities. Three hundred thousand seats to be sold. Average ticket price between $8 and $9. Some as high as $12.50. Oh, you bet it's going on.

But it's like Bob. You charge people $25 to see Evel Knievel jump over Snake River Canyon in a Skycycle, you better make sure Evel Knievel turns up and either blasts himself across that canyon or does the honourable thing and kills himself trying. Same as if you charge people $12.50 to see David Bowie in concert. You better make sure David Bowie turns up and blasts through the hits of David Bowie or kills himself trying. The bottom line: give 'em the show as promised on the ticket stub.

The show is not what's promised on the ticket stub.

The promise is clear. 'David Bowie'. He's that kooky English glitter-rocker who wears zany clothes and make-up. He may look faggy but he's *faaar-out*! He's a rock'n'roll magician, reaching out and sucking you inside his fantasy. He's an exorcist, ridding you of the demons of squaresville trying to turn your life into one long projectile vomit of sexless greyness. Like when he last toured just a few months ago, running around that screwball sci-fi city, hovering above the stalls on a crane and climbing inside that crazy diamond car with the giant hand inside it. Aw, man, he was *wild*! When Bowie comes to town it's like an air-raid siren going off

– *Come all ye freaks! Gooba gabba, gooba gabba!* A mass rally of space cadets gathering to hear the divine word of their glorious commander.

This is the promise. Ten dollars to see the spaceship land so they can all go home carrying moonbeams in a jar. Like it says, very clearly, on the ticket.

'DAVID BOWIE'.

Only the spaceship doesn't land.

Just a giant rug. A giant, *giant* plain white rug draped over what used to be the two Hunger City towers, curving down to the stage floor to provide the barest of backdrops.

Nor does their commander land.

What happens, instead, is this.

The cadets clomp to their seats, star-trekkin' rocky horrors in full facepaint trick and platform treat, when they see, on the stage, the giant rug. They think it could be hiding something. Maybe the spaceship they still believe is going to land. Maybe the rug is its landing pad? But whatever it is they know – it's Bowie! – so it's gonna be *out* of this freakin' world!

At the bottom, where the rug meets the stage, are amps and instruments. The cadets don't fully register their significance until his band walk on and a roaring excitement lasts as long as it takes everyone to realise it's *just* a band walking on. There are around a dozen of them, half of them singers, over half of them black and all looking pretty funky. So when they start singing about '*funky music!*' over funky music none of the cadets are too surprised. Just a little bored.

Then a little agitated. The funk turns to jazz and a scat duet of 'I'm In The Mood For Love' so hideous anyone not drowning it out with shrieks of 'WHERE'S BOWIE?' adds a clause in their will for those who are.

Then it gets worse. Jazz turns to soul, turns to jazzy soul, turns to The O'Jays' 'Love Train', turns to a sax solo, turns to Santana's 'Oye Cómo Va', turns to a bongo solo, turns to a wailing crescendo, turns to a gospel version of 'Memory Of A Free Festival' sounding like something from *Hair!* before David finally appears, sheepish as any groom half an hour late for his own wedding.

But, still! *There's* Bowie!

Or is it?

It's definitely him from the neck up. Tawny head, no eyebrows, face thin as a draughtsman's compass, even if the quiffy hair is frighteningly terrestrial. But the rest of him? Double-breasted bolero jacket, zoot suit slacks, chequered tie and braces. Dressed to croon. Which looked OK when he was gallivanting around Hunger City and hanging off cherry pickers. Less so in front of some Harlem Tabernacle Choir standing on a giant rug.

He does at least *sing* like Bowie. A Bowie having the devil cast out of him by that same tabernacle choir punching and kicking his songs to death with every weapon at their disposal. A sleazy sax that can't stop ejaculating, teeth-aching guitar solos and six alleged 'backing' vocalists who couldn't sing over David any more if they physically sat on his face. Gasping beneath are the likes of 'Rebel Rebel', 'Changes' and 'Suffragette City'. And these are the songs his space cadets *know*. Then come the ones they don't. The new Philadelphia songs. And they may be great songs, and they may be played by the best band capable of playing them since half the musicians who recorded them are the same musicians on the stage. But they're still unfamiliar, they're still soul songs pulling a stick-up job on a rock crowd and they still sound nothing like the David Bowie it says on their ticket. Just as that man on stage isn't the David Bowie it says on their ticket. He's a rasping James Milky Brown. An unripe Al Green. A Barry Too White. A black man trapped in a white body so thin you'd think it had TB.

Some fans still seem to love it, but then some fans love anything. Because they're fans. They're here watching Bowie and, for them, that's enough. But that's only *some* fans.

The rest?

All they see is David Bowie plummet to the depths of his own Snake River Canyon. As do the press.

'*Judging from the post-show mutterings of his disappointed hordes who'd come expecting some real flash and gotten little, his new style may be a rock and roll suicide move indeed.*'

'*Not only was the concert a letdown, but it was also a rip-off.*'

'*After all was said and done, I felt cheated.*'

'*His adoring fans were short-changed by the latest whim of David Bowie. Woefully so. Soul alone is not enough.*'

'*Take away the gimmicks and the glitter, drop the overt decadence, and what have you got left? Boredom.*'

Then that's the thing about the show. It always goes on. Even when it shouldn't.

THE DARKNESS. It, too, goes on, regardless of whether it shouldn't. The darkness does what the darkness likes. The darkness has no care, no fear, not even of light. The darkness is invincible. The darkness is everywhere. And, this year, *what* a show it's put on. Well, haven't *its* reviews in the press been amazing?

'PC BURIED PRETTY WIFE IN GARDEN'

'VOODOO DOLLS PUT MARK OF DEATH ON DETECTIVES'

'TINY SPECK OF LSD TURNED A MAN INTO A VAMPIRE'

'"SMELL OF DEATH" DRUG CRAZE HITS LONDON SCHOOLS'

'CAR PARK GANG RAPE GIRL, 14'

'EXORCIST MYSTERY OF DEATH FALL YOUTH'

'KNIFE CLUE TO BRIDE'S KILLER'

'MAMA CASS DEATH SHOCK'

'QUIET "MIDGET" MURDERS THREE'

'FAN TELLS OF HORROR AS BERNADETTE LAY DYING'

The darkness never lets up. Every day it tries its best to do its worst.

Take today, a typical autumnal Saturday, the papers hissing false promises for next week's general election – the second this year – Anthea giving Brucie a twirl at the top of the TV ratings and everybody 'Kung Fu Fighting' at number 1. And more music thrumming out of the pub jukebox in the Horse and Groom. Until 8.30 p.m. when the music stops. When everything stops. When a bomb explodes, injuring sixty and killing five: the youngest 17, the oldest 21. When darkness smothers Guildford.

As the screaming victims stumble out of the smoke and debris, 30 miles away in Muswell Hill a courting teenage couple are snuggling in the ABC for the late showing of *The Exorcist*. At 16, John shouldn't be watching an X certificate. Nor should his 15-year-old girlfriend, so disturbed she hides her face. 'Don't be silly,' teases John, 'there's nothing to be scared about.'

When it's finished he throws a gallant arm round her shoulders and walks her home where her mum makes them a cup of tea. They kiss goodnight on the doorstep. But it's only as he hurries back to his own house John can finally stop pretending. He has plenty to be scared about as he climbs into bed. The devil in Regan MacNeil and his own personal demon. The one called epilepsy waiting to strike as soon as he falls asleep. Making sure John never wakes up again.

This is what the darkness does. But it always knows it can do one better. Do even worse. And with time running out, with only so many weeks left before the bells of '75, after a performance as vile as this year's has been it still needs a crescendo. Before Christmas there will be more bombs, more rapes, more murders, more suicides – an avalanche of death and a tsunami of grief. But 1974 deserves something special. Something *really* dark. *Medieval*, even. Something nobody would ever believe possible in England in the latter years of the twentieth century.

On that same Saturday night. The night of the Guildford pub bomb. The night a teenage boy is frightened to death in a Muswell Hill cinema.

The night of the forty demons.

There is no cinema in Ossett. There used to be, but they demolished it to build a supermarket. And though there are many pubs to choose from, Michael doesn't drink in them. He's a stay-at-home kind of Yorkshireman, home being a semidetached corner of a cul-de-sac with his wife, Christine, and their five boys. A lot of mouths to feed and no time to be out of work with a bad back. Any other depressed unemployed farmhand would hit the bottle. But Michael's not a drinker. So he hits something else, just as potent, just as addictive. He hits God.

The worst kind of God. Not the normal going-to-church-every-Sunday God but the leaflets-in-the-street-and-banging-on-your-front-door God. The God of kneeling in strangers' living rooms, of insanity posing as piety, of mad-eyed young women pressing wooden crosses into his hand with 'Jesus Lives' printed on both sides before they roll around the carpet pretending to speak in tongues. The God that does no less damage to Michael's head than a pickaxe, that gives him seizures, that makes him sleep with the bedside lamp on all night because he's scared of the dark, that makes him think The Devil is telling him to kill himself. And all of this happens to Michael in the space of twelve days.

The twelfth day. That Saturday. Michael has been awake all night furiously crossing himself and babbling about Satan. One of his new God friends visits to take him and Christine out for a drive. They're barely out of the cul-de-sac when Michael screams like he's being electrocuted. If they had any sense, they'd take him to the nearest hospital or police station. But they don't. They take him to the nearest house of God.

A church on the outskirts of Barnsley and the vicarage of a Reverend Vincent and his wife. They've no sooner welcomed Michael shivering and moaning into their kitchen when he tips dinnerplates on the floor and attacks their cat. The vicar tries to intervene. Michael punches him in the face. The vicar's wife tells Christine there is an enormous force of evil emanating from her husband. Christine agrees. So does the vicar with his new black eye. It leaves them only one obvious course of action.

Exorcism.

The sort that requires a crack team of holy reinforcements. A local methodist minister and his wife and a fellow methodist lay preacher are summoned to join them. They read Bible passages aloud, sing hymns and pray until midnight brings the temporal sanctuary of the holy sabbath. Clutching Michael between them like arresting police officers, they drag him wailing and struggling out into the darkness, across the graveyard into the church vestry. There they carefully arrange hassocks on the floor in the shape of a cross. Michael is forced down and held down, one man to each thrashing limb. They grip tight, close their eyes and mumble Our Fathers.

The exorcism can now begin.

The evil spirit is asked to name itself.

'Incest!' says Michael.

The lay preacher crosses himself. 'Lord, hasten to our call for help and snatch from ruination and from the clutches of the noonday devil this human being made in your image and likeness.'

The preacher starts to chant. The others join in.

'The power of Christ compels you! The power of Christ compels you! The power of Christ compels you!'

Michael kicks, roars, whimpers, then drops silent. Demon Number One has been cast out. The vicar asks Michael if there are any more.

'Bestiality!' Demon Number Two.

Again, the crossing, the chanting, the power of Christ, the kicking, the screaming, the casting out.

'Blasphemy.' Three.

'Masochism.' Four.

'Heresy.' Five.

'Lewdness.' Six.

And so it goes on. Demon after demon for six hours of spasms and shrieking, of gibbering in tongues, of singing hymns, of sprinkling him with holy water, of forcing a crucifix in his mouth, of burning his wooden cross they decide is contaminated by The Devil. Until, by their count, forty separate demons have been cast out of Michael's body.

But by the cock crow of 7 a.m. the lay preacher remains troubled. Forty demons gone, but where was the one named 'Murder'? They still fear for Michael, still sick, still trembling. A call is made to Wakefield police station where the cells are stuffed with Saturday night's stewbums and the last thing any tired desk sergeant wants to hear is some cranky hooptedoodle about devils and exorcisms. When he refuses to send a car, the vicar's wife begs Christine to ring their family doctor as soon as they get home. 'But it's Sunday,' says Christine, shaking her head. 'And anyway, Michael would be annoyed.'

Half past eight, the hour of Stewpot's *Junior Choice* but no radio in the car as they're driven back to Ossett. To their semidetached house in the corner of the cul-de-sac where Michael and Christine are left alone. Their five boys are staying round the corner with their grandmother. It is just the two of them, their poodle and the suburban noiselessness of a Sunday morning. And that last demon.

The lay preacher was right. One left that they couldn't cast out. Because if they'd prayed that bit harder, then it wouldn't have happened.

Michael wouldn't have taken Christine up into their bedroom to tell his wife she was the root of all evil.

He wouldn't have gouged her eyes out with his fingers.

He wouldn't have torn her tongue out with his bare hands.

He wouldn't have dug his nails into her skin and peeled off her face like wrapping paper.

Christine Taylor wouldn't have died drowning in the inhalation of her own blood at the age of 29.

If they'd prayed harder, Michael wouldn't have stripped off all his clothes before walking down the stairs and wringing the poodle's neck.

He wouldn't have run out of his house, out of their cul-de-sac, a naked man smeared with his wife's blood now wearing her rings on his fingers.

He wouldn't have been found by the police in the middle of the road, cowering on his hands and knees, his forehead touching the tarmac.

Michael Taylor, 31, wouldn't have looked up into their disbelieving eyes and sobbed, 'I am covered with the blood of Satan.'

No, if they'd prayed that bit harder, this would never have happened. Not in a land of 'Annie's Song', instant mash and conveyor belts with cuddly toys. Not in God's own country. Not in England. Not in 1974.

EIGHTEEN

THE WORST HE CAN DO IS GREAT. That's what David says. What David firmly believes.

'The worst I can do is great. Sometimes I'm *incredible* but I'm never worse than great.'

Even if there are still some idiots who don't know it yet, the important thing is David does. If he didn't, then the reviews might actually hurt. The ones Corinne still brings him every morning in his suite in his new hotel, the Pierre, just a block up from his old one, the Sherry, with a similar view over the southeast corner of Central Park. The hotel his new friend was living in before he moved next door to Garbo, and what's good enough for Johnny Beatle is definitely good enough for Davey Bowie, back in New York bringing the show that shouldn't go on to Radio City Music Hall for a five-night stint. Five nights still boring fans with too many new songs they don't know, still ruining the old favourites they do, still mashing his jaw in the spotlight like he's chewing a glue sandwich that's pasting his gums to his lips. All that's changed is the encore, an easily imagined and even easier executed tack-on of the Stones' 'It's Only Rock 'N' Roll' to the end of 'Diamond Dogs' which he usually sings wearing a beret: it's only because American critics don't know who it is that none of them point out it makes him look like Frank Spencer.

What they *are* saying is bad enough. Three nights down, two to go, and this morning's *New York Times* isn't making the road any less bumpy. Eyes that last slept two changes of underwear ago scan the thin column on page 18.

'*Disappointing . . . lame . . . self-consciously uncomfortable . . . hoarse voice indeed.*'

David considers the words as a French pastry chef might consider a bluebottle diving towards his freshly glazed religieuse. He winces, closes the paper, pushes it away, shuts his eyes. Three moody seconds pass. He blinks them back open, a frown ploughing across his forehead. He sees the front page of the *Times* where he tossed it aside. A headline about the president of South Vietnam.

'MORE CRITICS ATTACK THIEU'

Critics attack. That's just what they do, isn't it? Attack! Attack! Attack! Even when everybody knows the worst he can do is great.

He turns to his bedside table. Next to the lamp are a razor blade and a curled banknote. David leans over and, each in their turn, finds a use for them both.

A sudden knock on the bedroom door. It pushes ajar. Corinne, her voice through the gap. 'David? The car'll be here in 30 minutes.'

The car?

Oh, god. The car. Yes, he remembers. He has another show to do. A television show, filming only a short distance from his hotel. But it's the middle of the day when he ought to be resting. For all the surgical instruments beside his bed, David is more tired than he looks, and he looks about as healthy as a child's chalked hopscotch grid after a night of heavy rain. Still, at least he always knows the very worst he can do is be great. As he tells himself, stooping once more over his bedside table.

'And, sometimes . . .' *Sniff.* '. . . I'm *incredible.*'

'**WHO IS HE?** What is he? Where did he come from? Is he a creature of a foreign power? Is he a creep? Is he dangerous? Is he smart? Dumb? Nice to his parents? Real? Put on? Crazy? Sane? Man? Woman? Robot? What *is* this?'

This is Dick Cavett introducing David Bowie to the stage of *The Dick Cavett Show*, a late-night talk show being prerecorded on a Saturday afternoon before a live audience in a small Broadway theatre now commandeered by ABC television as Studio TV-15.

And this is David Bowie, strolling past his band towards a microphone, a brown square-shouldered suit, blue shirt and Burberry check tie, a long fob chain dipping from belt to right trouser pocket, white shoes with argyle socks and flopping ducktail hair the colour of a tangerine that's been too long in the fruit bowl. His voice is coarse as pebbledash and by the time he's finished with '1984' its paintwork is hanging off in strips. 'Young Americans' is less of a strain, David more natural, more swinging, more lost inside the moment of the song, more delighting in the televisual shock of its jazzy newness, knowing when this is broadcast in another four weeks his fans watching at home still won't be able to buy it. Defries won't be happy, but right now Defries is out of the country because if he'd had his way David wouldn't even be *on* Dick's show for the same reason you won't ever see Elvis on Johnny Carson's. Which leaves his ever disobedient brand BOWIE live before network TV cameras completely off his leash. And off his head.

Dick sees it immediately. Or, rather, hears it.

The sniff.

Dick knows that sniff. Everyone in showbiz knows that sniff. Half the people watching at home will know that sniff. It makes Dick very uneasy because anyone with that sniff, *the* sniff, and you just never know what they're going to say or do on air. Which makes the next 15 minutes 15 of the more stressful minutes of Dick's televised life, squirming before the TV cameras and an excitable young crowd, attempting to tease some sense out of the unteasably insensible 5 foot 10 inch sniff called David Bowie.

The sniff alone wouldn't be so bad. The sniff plus the cane, that's what scares Dick. A black cane with a curved handle, like the kind Chaplin used to twiddle, suddenly appearing in David's left hand seconds before he plonks himself opposite in the vacant guest's chair. A knight of the dark arts brandishing an Excalibur of headfuckery.

David taps it noiselessly on the carpet beneath them. Rocks it gently side to side. Twists the handle top in circles. Slides his fingers down the shaft, raises it off the ground, lets it go then catches it before it reaches the floor. Draws lines through the carpet pile like it's a giant pencil. Hooks it round the back of his neck like trying to crook himself off stage. Brings it up to his mouth and kisses it. Scratches his head with it. Holds it lengthways with both hands like a curtain rail sliding his knuckles back and forth. Raps it against his knees. Raises it to his chin like an exercise bar. Strokes the shaft like he's wanking it. Runs his fingers along the curve like trying to peel a banana. Presses the tip down hard and pivots it like a pilot's joystick. Lays it down to take off his jacket. Chews his fingernails. Picks it up again and waves it in front of his face. Bites it between his teeth. Smooths his fingers over its surface like he's sculpting wet clay. Holds it like a steering wheel then stabs the ground hard like it's a gravedigger's spade. He does all of this between the constant sniffing, and grimacing, and biting his tongue, and contorting his lips, and skewing his jaw, and baring clenched teeth like Cheeta the chimpanzee for the duration of Dick's kid-gloved cross-examination. The sum of his extractions being that David is not academic, says 'nicked' when he means stolen, gets nervous when asked if he's nervous, is scared of flying, has natural blond hair, a dead father and a mother he's not close to who pretends he isn't hers, likes the photography of Diane Arbus, is fascinated with the theory of black noise capable of destroying whole cities, may or may not be writing a novel based on his travels on the Trans-Siberian Express, has no mission statement, is not an intellectual, doesn't like talking politics, thinks all rock stars are 'pretty nutty to be doing it in the first place', ultimately sees himself as a storyteller, doesn't really care what anyone else says and likes fiddling with his cane because 'it's therapeutic'.

The cane is still in his hands when he rejoins the band for his new funked-up medley of two R&B oldies, 'Foot Stomping' and 'I Wish I Could Shimmy Like My Sister Kate', now the baton of a regular song-and-dance man putting on his ritz with a basalt growl, a harem in his pants and a flea circus in his gums, his addictions never more terrifyingly transparent than here, now, as he is or soon will be on American network television firing through the same electron gun as President Ford and Richie Cunningham. An audaciously saucy, faggy-limbed, eyebrowless English freak dressed like a 1930s flesh peddler, spitting filthy black soul in the spluttering face of a moustachioed white America thumbing its belt loops to Bachman-Turner Overdrive. Behold, the new red under the bed. The *real* space invader. The scary disco hipster from Planet Blow.

Which all makes this time one of those *sometimes*. He is. Incredible.

★

HE SHOULD WRITE A SONG ABOUT IT. If anyone could, Bruce could. It's got everything he could ever want in a song. Hitching rides, bus depot bums, downtown diners, troubadours, rock'n'roll, dark nights of the soul and strange characters. *Really* strange characters. What would he call it?

'12th Street Supposedly Sunday (Barry)'.

Opening with a guitar in G flat and a descending piano.

'Sleeping off the witches when a telephone screamed . . .'

Starting with the night before when he played Salem, riding back through the wee small hours to Jersey in his band's tour bus he calls the colour of '*Exorcist* green', hitting the pillow as dawn's first light skims over the Atlantic. The last thing he needs that groggy Sunday is a noon wake-up call, but how is Ed to know? Ed, a disc jockey in Philly and as big a supporter of Bruce as anyone with an aerial will find on their FM dial. Only three weeks ago he'd had him on his show the day after Bruce's run at the Tower, when Ed previewed a new track from his unfinished third album called 'Born To Run'. It was the first time Bruce had heard what it sounds like on the radio because it was the first time anyone had ever played it. And it was that same show when Ed asked him about the rumours David Bowie had recorded one of his songs.

'Supposedly, y'know,' drawled Bruce in a voice so sleepy any listener would think Ed was stood over him swinging a pocket watch. 'I haven't heard it yet. He supposedly did "Saint In The City" and "Growin' Up".'

Supposedly is what ruins Bruce's lie-in. Ed's just learned David is back in Philly for a week finishing the album he began in August. His producer just rang him to ring Bruce to drag him down tonight so he can finally hear what the supposedly David has been up to.

Which is where the second verse would pick up a gear.

'Thumbways to Trailways, got no need for gas . . .'

About how Bruce doesn't have a car so has to hitch to Asbury Park then catch a bus the remaining 70 miles, describing his fellow passengers, the soldier on furlough, the old lady in the brown coat, the stumbling drunk reeking of Old Harper same as the winos in the Filbert Street terminal where Bruce finally falls off in the poet's hour before midnight.

'And the tramps they're all shinin' bright as carnival lights . . .'

He's met by Ed who takes him to the studio a few blocks away on 12th Street. A chilly November night the week before Thanksgiving,

146

they're not expecting the half-dozen high-school kids huddling outside the entrance. Bruce gently steps over them, an anonymous shadow with a Serpico beard, scruffy jeans and splotchy brown leather jacket. For all they care he could be the pizza man.

'Cold as stone angels, the brats of desire . . .'

Now we'd get to the heart of the song. Because when Bruce arrives in Sigma, David isn't even there. It's just his producer, Tony, and a few stray musicians laying down overdubs. Time for a little more fire in his voice.

'Don't deal from the bottom, Jack, my ticket's return . . .'

At this point it could do with a saxophone solo from The Big Man. Something to drag out the suspense before the next verse when, just after 1 a.m., David finally shows. A dramatic pause where the music stops. Then a count in of 'one-two-three', snare drum, take it away.

'A subway Lon Chaney, he was shakin' with dust . . .'

Is how Bruce might describe him. Because he's expecting 'weird' but not a chalky zombie in a beret and red braces holding up baggy black pants, eyes sparkling with his own peculiar embalming fluid.

'But, boy, you shoulda heard this undead Johnny rap . . .'

Which is what they do. Which is *all* they do. Talk, on and off, for the best part of three hours. Bruce hears all about the time David first saw him last year in Max's, how his songs knocked him out, how Bruce is the only American singer-songwriter David can think of whose work he'd want to record. And for maybe the first hour or so, while they stick to the subject of music, it's all very sweet. Until the topic shifts. To flying saucers. David is very eager to tell Bruce, to tell anyone, about the US government's smokescreen around a recent UFO crash in Ohio where they secretly recovered the bodies of four aliens. 'All three feet tall,' says David, 'with giant brains.'

Bruce has his chorus.

'So long, spaceman, I ain't sorry I came,

But there's a waitress down on Broad Street and she's callin' my name . . .'

Is more or less how it pans out. Bruce lasts until 5 a.m. when, hitch-beat and Bowied out, he and Ed leave to grab some much needed breakfast. The funny thing being that after travelling all this way, he never does hear David's version of 'It's Hard To Be A Saint In The City'. When the time comes to gather round and press play, David suddenly decides it isn't ready. Supposedly.

'*Supposedly Sunday, he'd sing me my song . . .*'

And that's maybe the drum-rolling end of it?

Except the payoff is all in the last verse. Where Bruce stays in Philly that night so he and Ed can see David's show at the local ice hockey stadium. About as bad a show-that-shouldn't-have-gone-on as David's played all tour. So bad that the moment it's over they hop in a cab to catch another friend of Ed's at the Academy of Music, Billy Joel, who later joins them for a midnight bite at the diner across the street. And you'll *never* believe who else is there . . .

No, not David. That'd be *way* too corny a song. No, it's another friend of Ed's – Barry Manilow – here in Philly to promote his new single 'Mandy'. So the next thing they're all pulling up chairs at the same table, Bruce, Billy and Barry, three very different singers swapping stories of chasing riches and the trials of the road. Billy, in town touring his third album. Bruce, working hard on his own third album he knows will be make-or-break. And Barry, well, he's under no illusion. Last week he sold out Carnegie Hall. He tells Bruce and Billy straight. 'I'm going to be the biggest star out of anyone sat at this table.'

So there's the punchline. Bruce Springsteen hitches all the way to Philadelphia to meet David Bowie only to end up ego-slapped by Barry Manilow.

'. . . *Supposedly one day, bigger than King Kong.*'

It really would make a great number. Maybe not as good as 'Born To Run'. Maybe not even as good as 'Mandy', but still.

'12th Street Supposedly Sunday (Barry)'.

Who knows. Bruce may write it yet.

NINETEEN

THIS CITY DON'T NEED NO SAINTS. The only one who can save you here is yourself. Over seven-and-a-half million people but whatever their religion it doesn't matter. They've all the churches, synagogues, mosques and temples they need but once they're up off their knees when they step back out on the streets not one of them has a prayer. How can you ask any god for protection from a city that if they were doing their job properly wouldn't exist in the first place? No, here in New York you have to save your own soul. Build your own heaven. Dig your own hell.

None deeper than Downtown, where it looks like a war's just ended and that war lost. A city that must've been bombed into surrender as what else but heavy weaponry could have torn up the roads with so many potholes. And those must be the victims, the slobbering maniacs with blood gushing from their foreheads, limping into the traffic with just the one shoe on, clinging for dear life to the nearest chain-link fence while they shit or puke or both simultaneously. More sprawling flat on the sidewalk, still as corpses, which some of them are, run over by Night Train or tossed out with junk but not a sinner among them with the nerve to ask to be *saved*. Just flopping on the Bowery, pissing themselves to death, blind as mannequins to the skinny legs of young life marching over them to a club that smells almost as bad as they do. But then nobody goes to CBGB's for the aroma.

They go to see and hear the tomorrow they know is theirs. Because it's the end of '74 and, baby, here in New York you can literally hear the decade snapping in half. A fast clean break called the Ramones – four kids from Queens, thin as toothpicks, loud as hammer drills. And if not them at CBGB's, then similar vibrations round the corner in Club 82, a plush velvet trannie bar run by Butch and Tommy, two lesbians the size of dumper trucks, where even David's limo has been known to roll up just long enough so its axles don't end up on bricks to marvel at the scuttle bug guitars of Television.

In these, the city's ashiest slums, there are phoenixes rising. Joey, Johnny, Dee Dee and Tommy, the four horsemen of the fuzzpocalypse. The six-stringed escapologist called Tom Verlaine. A scarecrow-like Boudica called Patti Smith. The forces sweetheart of a dimestore army called Debbie Harry. Because rock'n'roll isn't dead, only broken. And, just like ABC's new *Six Million Dollar Man*, they can rebuild it.

Though none of them are here hurdling over dead bums tonight, this week before Christmas. And there's no sign of David either, least not on the Bowery.

To find him we need to go *waaay* uptown. There's always the subway, if you can handle so much graffiti you'll feel you're riding inside an aerosol can, and the stench, and the claustrophobia, and the groping afterwork drunks, and the packhorse shoppers drowning in Gimbels bags, and the chance you'll be mugged by a 12-year-old, if not in your car then when you reach your station. But better to stay above ground. To see, smell and hear the city as it is, in winter, after the rain, in the dark. The icy northwesterly wind in your bones, the stink of dogshit and roach spray ebbing into diesel and burnt onions as you follow the star of the Empire State.

Heading up along Broadway, the cries of 'loose joints' hawking a dollar's worth of ready-rolled getting louder the closer we get to the Garden. Loose trade is booming tonight because Georgie Beatle is playing, which means Johnny Beatle will be there, and if David could only decide which of John's hips he should join himself to he'd be there with him. And would, if only he hadn't crossed George's path backstage at a gig in Memphis last month when he'd pulled David's hat off. 'I wanna take a good look at you,' said George, 'because you always look so dopey in all those photos.' The quiet ones are always the worst.

So let's assume John's there, and not UFO spotting on the roof next to Garbo, but David isn't. And keep walking, up through the 30s into the 40s, every block the hookers growing younger, the hawkers uglier, the neon brighter till you can't see your feet for the dazzle of electricity. Only three weeks since Macy's parade when Bullwinkle and Snoopy floated above Times Square but now it's all *Death Wish* and *The Godfather Part II*. No David to be found round here, other than in the racks of King Karol or Sam Goody where *David Live* has just fallen out of the national Top 10. And no Mick Ronson either. The giant Mainman billboard that made him look like David Cassidy is gone. Same as the not-so-giant Mainman play. The one called *Fame*, based on the life of Marilyn Monroe, which opened just down there on a Monday night in mid-November at the Golden Theater. And closed, just down there on a Monday night in mid-November at the Golden Theater. One night, one house, one performance: estimated company loss to David and Defries, a quarter of a million dollars.

We could try looking for Defries too but we'd be wasting our time. Head up and eastwards to Park Avenue and we'll find the Mainman office closed for the holidays. Nothing there but plants dying of thirst, the ghostly smell of dead cigars and a cemetery of an in-tray, piled high with the paper headstones of that doomed Broadway play and the careers of Ronson and Dana Gillespie. All Defries had to do this year was 'sell Bowie'. All Defries sold this year *was* Bowie. All Defries has next year *is* Bowie. But, if nothing else, he still does. At least that's the thought blowing a smoke ring on a plane bound for sunny Mustique, where he'll be ringing in the New Year two thousand hammock-swinging miles away from subzero Manhattan. Yes, *at least* he still does. At least so he thinks.

Must be something about Christmastime that scares every devil out of the city. Now that the days are at their shortest and the darkness at its darkest you won't find *The Exorcist* anywhere. Its last projection here was back in July. The nearest thing to a film about a possessed female is *A Woman Under the Influence* up at the Columbia on 64th. Give it another year, and the same screen will be flickering with a different insanity when New York gets its overdue taste of *Stardust*. But that's not the lonely English rock star strung out in his castle we're looking for tonight. Double back a few blocks, turn right and follow the sirens towards the park. There, up on the corner, in the Pierre Hotel. That's *our* Jim MacLaine.

But then it all depends how we look at him.

So here's David, alone in his suite, dropping ash as he bends over a dining table arranging tiny cut-out paper figures in a little model clay city. He's got names for them all – 'Halloween Jack', 'Maggie the Lion', 'Charge', 'Harpie' – and a bulky video camera he's hired so he can film them, and a script somewhere within the chaos of notepads at his feet set sometime around the year 2020, when he imagines we'll all be rioting on rollerskates and living on processed rations of 'mealcaine'. We can see all this, and over there the mirror, and the razor, and the banknote, and the ashtray somewhere beneath the slag heap of filter tips, and the empty bottle of Courvoisier, and the granite eyeballs of a man who hasn't slept in days, and the body no heavier and its limbs no thicker than his camera tripod, and we could easily believe that this is the lying-in-the-bath-with-his-clothes-on Jim MacLaining end of it. The one he's always known was coming.

The only performance that makes it, that really makes it, that makes it all the way, is the one that achieves madness. Right?

All the way. A flipped-out rock star, lost and alone, shut away in his sad make-believe paper-puppet prison, one last kiss of his white demon from the overdose, the ambulance, tomorrow's front-page headline. Christmas cancelled for 1974 because 'DAVID BOWIE IS DEAD'.

But life isn't always like the movies, is it?

Take another look at David. In a few days' time the decade will tip like a seesaw into part two. And here he is, already plotting fifty years ahead of the odd misshapen world outside his window, an artist unshackled, master of his own universe with no one to stop him, no one to tell him who he should be or what he should do. Because as David presses his sharp sleepless eye to the camera viewfinder he doesn't see pieces of paper and blobs of clay. He sees the future.

The Seventies' future. His future.

And why shouldn't his itchy lips smack and his lusty heart pump as he presses the record button. Knowing he's the only one directing it.

EPILOGUE

IT'S GONE. Not Jilly's itself. That's still there, a whippet's piss from Piccadilly station down the bottom of Gore Street, but now 'under new management'. No more Bowie Night. Just 'Disco Dancing', strictly Friday to Sunday, 15p a pint and the same for a Snowball.

There are, of course, alternatives. For 'luxury' there's Annabell's. For 'naughty people, nice sounds' there's Tramps. For 'the sophisticated set' there's the 97 Club. If you want to 'bump your baby to the latest bumping sounds', there's Rafters. And, girls, Wednesday's your lucky night in Waves – 'Free Before 11.30!' – just as it is over in Pip's. No tie, no entry, Trophy bitter and copping a feel to Disco-Tex & The Sex-O-Lettes. This is Manchester, but in December 1974 this could be anywhere.

Anywhere in Discotannia.

It isn't David's country anymore. It isn't Harold Wilson's either, even after two narrow election wins in less than eight months. And it's definitely not Marc Bolan's, now a tax exile in Monaco whose latest single didn't even scuff the Top 40. Nor is it Lord Lucan's, the Cresta bear's, Theo Kojak's or even the Bay City Rollers' – the only ones who could stop *David Live* from becoming his fourth number 1 album. It's not anyone's. Just a nanny-murdering, frothy, man, who loves ya baby, shang-a-lang-ing no man's land.

But that doesn't mean it's forgotten him.

The pop mailbags still spill with letters from his staunchest fans, even if they're mostly like Nick in Wandsworth moaning: '*Why is it that the USA gets all the attention when it comes to Bowie?*' Not a week goes by without another new headline speculating on when he *will* return to Britain: '*definitely in the spring,*' says the *NME*; '*a mammoth extravaganza at Wembley Stadium,*' says the *Maker*; '*around the same time he releases his new album,* Fascination,' guesses *Record Mirror*. You'll still find his name in a *19* magazine feature on bisexuality and a story in the *Express* about a hip young stonemason rebuilding Canterbury Cathedral whose workshop is postered with Ziggy. He's still keeping the jigsaw fingers of police photofitters busy – the latest, a bank robber in Glasgow '*with prominent cheekbones, a gaunt long face which was very pale and dirty fair wavy hair in a David Bowie style*'. There are still plenty of boys with shaved eyebrows and one earring still being easily confused with girls just like them wearing the exact same shade of blusher. And everywhere you breathe, north or south, there is still glitter in the air. Only now it's a different kind.

It's not the sort you see anymore, except on a ball twirling above a dancefloor. More the sort you hear, like the whisper of a magic spell. An abracadabra to get up and get down. A sound that's been bewitching the number 1 spot on and off since the summer, first George McCrae and the Three Degrees, more recently 'Sad Sweet Dreamer' and the first, last and everything of Barry White. Black music born of a light fantastic. Whatever it takes to fight the darkness.

Oh, *it's* still there. Sucking the last dregs from '74's cup of abominations in bread strikes, more pub bombings and young brides strangled on their way home carrying never-to-be-wrapped Christmas presents. So is *The Exorcist*, now in its fortieth sickbag-popping week at the Scene 4 on Wardour Street. Next to it, Scene 2, where five times a day teenage girls temporarily forget David Essex is alive and well and the biggest-selling male singles artist of the year as they grizzle into their tissues for dead Jim MacLaine. But then *Stardust* is only a fiction. The credits will roll, the seats will flip up and their tears won't have filled anything more than a Smarties lid.

In Stockwell, they've burst dams. The first Christmas without Bernadette is like burying her all over again. Six months since the

Whelans did, the desecrations of her grave have already been too many. The wreaths not yet wilted, the rock singer Michael des Barres, formerly of Silverhead, announced he'd written a song about her: 'Teenybopper Death (He Loves You Bernadette)'. Though never actually released, it was still a minor hit in the charts of tabloid upset. 'How can these people be so heartless and unconcerned?' asked her dad, just as Bell Records released a souvenir LP of David Cassidy's last tour of Britain, much of it recorded at White City. Not content with killing a teenage girl, they kept the tape rolling and stuck it in a cardboard sleeve to be sold with a free poster. *Cassidy Live!* A homicide crime scene at 33⅓.

There's another just up the stairs in their Crowhurst House maisonette. Bernadette's bedroom, still untouched. On the wall, still, the posters of her David, the last thing she saw before closing the door and walking to her death. On the bed, still, the records she laid out the morning of the day she was murdered. And outside her window, still, that infinite malicious mocking darkness.

The same darkness pressing against the panes of a first-floor flat in Beckenham. On the other side of the glass another mother, sitting all alone with a cigarette in her hand. Not grieving, just grumbling.

Christmas time and Peggy Jones's youngest still hasn't rung. He never rings. Only his wife, Angela. Monstrous strumpet that she is, last week flashing her Janet Reger knickers all over the papers again. But at least she *rings*. Lets Peggy know how her grandson is doing and how 'FAAABULOUS' his new Scottish nanny is. But David? Not a peep. Never tells her anything. Not even that he's just been on American television telling the world he's never been particularly close to his mother. And how would she feel if he did? 'We have an understanding,' he'd said. But her David is the one thing Peggy's never understood.

Doesn't he *ever* think about his family? About his half-brother still in the local mental hospital, Terry, so loyal and loving, to her, and to David? Doesn't he sometimes wonder how Terry's doing? Doesn't he care how *she* is doing? Whether she's alright? Whether she might be lonely this Christmas, pulling her own cracker to 'Lonely This Christmas'? Doesn't he ever worry how she copes all by herself on her old age pension? Eleven pounds fifty a week! And doesn't he ever stop to realise she's now been a widow *five* years?

This August the fifth, did he even remember? Five years since his father died. Five years since they scattered his ashes in a crematorium rose garden in Elmers End. David, then just 22 and still living at home, not yet married, not yet a father, not yet famous. Only *five years* ago. And now look at him, on the front page of *The Sun* embracing Elizabeth Taylor. *Her* David! Well, didn't *that* say it all! No time to ring his poor mum, too busy groping Liz *'glowingly beautiful in a sapphire Mexican kaftan'*. Funny how people can change so much in as little as five years. And, god only knows, nobody's changed more in that time than her David.

Peggy stubs her cigarette out in a glass ashtray crowded with the twisted bodies of similarly slain Embassy Filters and automatically lights another. Beside her, the telephone still not ringing next to a picture of her son, aged 12, in his school blazer and tie. Opposite on the living-room wall an even larger framed picture of her son, a dreamy curly-haired 22. In the corner, the television yammering with *Sale of the Century* next to the pile of her son's records.

And outside, the black of a winter's night reflecting her moping scowl straight back at her. She winces, rising from her armchair, shuffling in her slippers the short distance to the windowsill. Staring back from the glass, in her eyes, her son's eyes. The child. The man. The stranger.

We were never that close particularly. We have an understanding.

Then with a violent tug Peggy pulls the curtains tight. Shutting out the darkness.

Which is all she or anyone can do. Try to keep at bay that which we can never beat, merely learn to withstand. The demon we know is always out there, banging to be let in. But just because it is, doesn't mean we have to. And just because we don't have to, doesn't mean in our own weird and terrible way, deep down, we still need it, if only to better appreciate the light. Because if David's mum could just peek out and look up, she'd be able to see for herself. If it wasn't for all that darkness, how else would we separate the stars?

BOWIEDISCOGRAPHY74

January   **LULU**
             'The Man Who Sold The World'
             b/w 'Watch That Man'
             Polydor 2001 490. Both sides written, arranged★ and produced★
             by David who also provides saxophone and backing vocals. Reached
             number 3 in February. ★Mick Ronson co-credited.

February   **'Rebel Rebel'**
             b/w 'Queen Bitch'
             RCA Victor LPBO 5009. Peaked at number 5 for two weeks in
             early March.

March   **MICK RONSON**
             Slaughter On 10th Avenue
             'Love Me Tender', 'Growing Up And I'm Fine'★, 'Only After
             Dark', 'Music Is Lethal'★ / 'I'm The One', 'Pleasure Man'–
             'Hey Ma Get Pa'★, 'Slaughter On 10th Avenue'
             RCA Victor APL1 0353. Solo debut from ex-Spiders guitarist most
             notable for its three songs★ with music and/or lyrics specially provided
             by David. Entered the chart at number 9 the same month.

STEELEYE SPAN
Now We Are Six
Chrysalis CHR 1053. *David plays guest alto saxophone on a cover of the Phil Spector Teddy Bears' classic 'To Know Him Is To Love Him'. The album reached number 13 in April.*

DANA GILLESPIE
Weren't Born A Man
RCA Victor APL1 0354. *Includes two tracks produced and arranged by David and Mick Ronson originally recorded in July 1971 for a shared promo LP funded by Gem management: Dana's version of David's 'Andy Warhol' (also issued as a single in August '74, RCA 2446); and her own composition 'Mother, Don't Be Frightened'. The rest of the album was recorded much later without any involvement from David.*

April   **'Rock 'N' Roll Suicide'**
b/w 'Quicksand'
RCA Victor LPBO5021. *Chronologically anomalous single release of 1972* Ziggy Stardust *album track. Significant as the first to credit David as simply 'Bowie' on the label, setting a precedent for the rest of his releases on RCA this year. Reached number 22 in early May.*

May   ***Diamond Dogs***
'Future Legend', 'Diamond Dogs', 'Sweet Thing', 'Candidate', 'Sweet Thing (Reprise)', 'Rebel Rebel' / 'Rock 'N' Roll With Me', 'We Are The Dead', '1984', 'Big Brother', 'Chant Of The Ever Circling Skeletal Family'
RCA Victor APLI 0576. *First album to be wholly written, arranged and produced by David. Entered the UK chart at number 1 in the first week of June where it stayed for four weeks.*

June   **'Diamond Dogs'**
b/w 'Holy Holy'
RCA Victor APBO 0293. *B-side is the infinitely superior remake of David's flop 1971 single, as recorded with The Spiders From Mars*

and originally intended for the Ziggy Stardust *album. Reached number 21 in mid-July.*

September   **'Knock On Wood'**
b/w 'Panic In Detroit'
RCA Victor 2466. Both sides recorded live at the Tower Theater, Philadelphia. Reached number 10 in October.

October   ***David Live***
'1984', 'Rebel Rebel', 'Moonage Daydream', 'Sweet Thing' / 'Changes', 'Suffragette City', 'Aladdin Sane', 'All The Young Dudes', 'Cracked Actor' / 'When You Rock 'N' Roll With Me'★, 'Watch That Man', 'Knock On Wood', 'Diamond Dogs' / 'Big Brother', 'The Width Of A Circle', 'The Jean Genie', 'Rock 'N' Roll Suicide'
RCA Victor APL2 0771. David's first official live (and first double) album. All tracks recorded at the Tower Theater, Philadelphia. Entered the UK chart at number 2 in mid-November. ★Title as listed on sleeve.

BOWIESOURCES74

VARIOUS AUTHOR INTERVIEWS conducted for the *Bowie Odyssey* series; for this book particular thanks to Patti Brett and Chris Charlesworth. Additional information from this author's past interviews with Carlos Alomar and Tony Visconti (both 2006).

The memoirs of Angie Bowie, *Free Spirit* (Mushroom Books, 1981) and *Backstage Passes: Life on the Wild Side with David Bowie* (with Patrick Carr, Putnam, 1993); Amanda Lear, *My Life with Dali* (Virgin, 1985); Geoff MacCormack with foreword by David Bowie, *From Station to Station: Travels with Bowie 1973 – 1976* (Genesis, 2007) and *David Bowie: Rock 'N' Roll With Me* (ACC Editions, 2023); Terry O'Neill, *Bowie by O'Neill* (Cassell, 2019); Cherry Vanilla, *Lick Me: How I Became Cherry Vanilla* (Chicago Review Press, 2010); Tony Visconti, *Bowie, Bolan and the Brooklyn Boy* (HarperCollins, 2007); and Tony Zanetta, as detailed in his and Henry Edwards' *Stardust: The David Bowie Story* (McGraw-Hill, 1986).

The chronology of Bowie historian Kevin Cann's *Any Day Now: David Bowie: The London Years 1947–74* (Adelita, 2010).

Other works: David Buckley, *Strange Fascination: Bowie: The Definitive Story* (Virgin, 2000); William S. Burroughs, *The Wild Boys* (Penguin Classics, 2008); David Cassidy, *Could it be Forever? – My Story* (Headline, 2007); Ray Connolly, *Stardust* (Fontana, 1974); Neil Cossar, *David*

Bowie: I Was There (Red Planet, 2017); David Essex, *Over the Moon: My Autobiography* (Virgin, 2012); Peter & Leni Gillman, *Alias David Bowie* (New English Library, 1987); Paul Gorman, *The Life & Times of Malcolm McLaren: The Biography* (Constable, 2020); Roger Griffin, *David Bowie: The Golden Years* (Omnibus Press, 2016); C. David Heyman, *Liz: An Intimate Biography of Elizabeth Taylor* (Heinemann, 1995); Jerry Hopkins, *Bowie* (MacMillan, 1985); Dylan Jones, *David Bowie: A Life* (Windmill Books, 2018); Kitty Kelley, *Elizabeth Taylor: The Last Star* (Simon & Schuster, 1981); Wendy Leigh, *Bowie: The Biography* (Gallery Books, 2016); Cliff McLenehan, *Marc Bolan: 1947–1977 A Chronology* (Helter Skelter, 2002); Chris O'Leary, *Rebel Rebel: All the Songs of David Bowie from '64 to '76* (Zero Books, 2015); May Pang with Henry Edwards, *Loving John* (Corgi, 1983); Mark Paytress, *Bolan: The Rise and Fall of a 20th Century Superstar* (Omnibus Press, 2006); Guy Peellaert and Nik Cohn, *Rock Dreams* (Pan, 1974); Nicholas Pegg, *The Complete David Bowie* (expanded and updated edition) (Titan Books, 2016); Walter Ross, *The Immortal* (Frederick Muller, 1958); Bruce Springsteen, *Born to Run* (Simon & Schuster, 2016); Paul Trynka, *Iggy Pop: Open Up and Bleed* (Sphere, 2008) and *Starman: David Bowie: The Definitive Biography* (Sphere, 2012); Pete Waterman, *I Wish I Was Me: The Autobiography* (Virgin, 2000); Andrew Yule, *Enigma: David Puttnam, The Story so Far* (Mainstream Publishing, 1988).

Key period broadcasts and theatrical releases referenced: *The Exorcist* (Hoya Productions, 1973), directed by William Friedkin, screenplay by William Peter Blatty; *Stardust* (Goodtime Enterprises, 1974), directed by Michael Apted, screenplay by Ray Connolly.

Period newspapers and magazines. National: *Daily Mirror, Daily Express, Daily Mail, Daily Telegraph, Guardian, News of the World, Nova, Observer, Radio Times, The Sun, Sunday Express, Sunday Mirror, Sunday People, Sunday Times* (and *Magazine*), *The Times, TV Life, TV Times, The Universe, Vogue.* Regional: *Belfast Telegraph, Birmingham Evening Mail, Birmingham Post, Cambridge Evening News, Chelsea News, Coventry Evening Telegraph, Daily Mail* (Hull), *Daily Record* (Scotland), *Evening Chronicle* (Newcastle), *Evening News* (London), *Evening Post* (Nottingham), *Evening Post* (Reading), *Evening Standard* (London), *Evening Times* (Glasgow), *Fulham Chronicle, Glamorgan Gazette, Hampstead & Highgate Express, Hornsey Journal, Irish Independent, Kensington News and Post, Liverpool Daily*

Post, *Liverpool Echo, Luton News, Manchester Evening News, Middlesex County Times & Gazette, New Milton Advertiser, North Devon Journal-Herald, Ossett Observer, Press and Journal* (Aberdeen), *South Kensington News & Chelsea Post, South London Press, Sunday Sun* (Newcastle), *Western Daily Press.*

Pop/rock and teenage: *Disc, Fabulous 208* (as *Fabulous 208 & Hit* from mid-January '74; as *Fabulous 208 & Hit & Melanie* from November '74), *Honey & Vanity Fair, Jackie, Look-In, Look Now, Melody Maker, Mirabelle* (as *Mirabelle with Valentine* from November '74), *Music Scene* (ceased/merged with *Fan* October '74), *Music Week, New Musical Express, 19, Popswop, Record Mirror* (as *Record and Radio Mirror* from January to August '74; as *Record and Popswop Mirror* from September '74), *Romeo* (ceased/merged with *Diana* September '74), *Sounds, Valentine* (ceased/merged with *Mirabelle* November '74); with very special thanks to the archives of Tom Sheehan.

Counterculture, gay/women's lib: *Gay News, Spare Rib, Time Out.*

North American publications: *Billboard, Boston Globe, Cashbox, Circus Raves, Creem, The Drummer, Hit Parader, Indianapolis Star, Los Angeles Times, Memphis Commercial Appeal, Minneapolis Star, Minneapolis Tribune, Montreal Star, New York Times, Ottawa Citizen, Ottawa Journal, Philadelphia Daily News, Philadelphia Inquirer, Philadelphia Weekly, Rolling Stone, Sarasota Herald-Tribune, Sarasota Journal, Time, TV Guide, Variety, Village Voice, Wisconsin State Journal.*

For extra help and facilitating, thanks to Kevin Cummins, Bob Gruen, Laurence Myers, Shrene Hudson at South London Crematorium and the Catholic Archdiocese of Southwark.

BOWIE**IMAGES**74

FRONT COVER
Who can he be now? David regenerates in America, 1974 (Paperback © Michael Ochs Archives/Getty; Hardback special edition © Bettmann/Getty).

IMAGES page 1
The cane mutiny. A powder keg of weird waiting to detonate on *The Dick Cavett Show*, Studio TV-15, West 58th Street, New York City, 2 November 1974 (© Ann Limongello/Getty).

IMAGES pages 2–3
Darkness, 1974. Clockwise from top left: Marc Bolan, possessed (© Pictorial Press Ltd/Alamy); Friends Heather and Valerie prove not everyone who sees *The Exorcist* leaves the cinema in an ambulance on its opening day in London's Leicester Square, 14 March 1974 (© Tom King/Daily Mirror/Mirrorpix); The Devil in David Bowie (eyes/top © Michael Ponomareff/Ponopresse/Getty; teeth/bottom © Gijsbert Hanekroot/Alamy); The forty demons in Michael Taylor (© Keystone Press/Alamy); Hell is a daughter's empty bedroom for the Whelans of Stockwell, 27 May 1974 (© PA Images/Alamy).

IMAGES pages 4–5
The man who fell. David drops into the darkness, October 1974 (© Michael Ochs Archives/Getty).

IMAGES pages 6-7
Bowietannia, 1974. Top left: The Three Degrees force David's year of decision (© Pictorial Press Ltd/Alamy). **Bottom left:** Wet and not getting any dryer, David Essex as Jim MacLaine in *Stardust* (© Studio Canal/ Shutterstock). **Centre:** Nuclear (war) family – the Joneses in Amsterdam, February 1974 (© Pictorial Press Ltd/Alamy). **Top right:** Bruce Lee sends the kids double kung fu crazy in *Enter the Dragon* (© Landmark Media/Alamy). **Bottom right:** Wanted! A 1974 police photofit of a child sex attacker described as having a hairstyle 'like David Bowie' (Author's collection).

IMAGES page 8
To reach the unreachable star. David bares his soul on the stage of New York's Radio City Music Hall, November 1974 (© Bettmann/Getty).

ENDPAPERS
Ground control. David, RCA Studios, New York City, May 1974 (© Michael Ochs Archives/Getty).

Picture research and layout concept by Simon Goddard.

THANKYOU

A mighty run up the Rocky steps for Patti Brett in Philadelphia.

A 'loose joint!' for Chris Charlesworth,
heart still somewhere in New York City, 1974.

A deafening chant for the ever circling Omnibus family:
David Barraclough, Claire Browne, Greg Morton,
David Stock and Debra Geddes at Great Northern PR.

Making a deal like no other candidate,
Kevin Pocklington at the North Literary Agency.

If it's gonna be me, then it's gotta be Alison Rae,
the best copy-editor in Bowietannia or elsewhere.

And to Sylv – who never sang 'Y Viva Espana' in 1974,
though she's just as lovely as the Sylvia who did.

DAVID BOWIE
will return in

BOWIEODYSSEY**75**

COMING 2025